Messages from Gaia

Wisdom and Love from our Earth Mother

Mary Kirkpatrick

Copyright © 2010 Mary Jane Crooks

Interior and cover images by Andrew Crooks

All rights reserved. No part of this book may be used or reproduced by any means, graphic, electronic, or mechanical, including photocopying, recording, taping or by any information storage retrieval system without the written permission of the publisher except in the case of brief quotations embodied in critical articles and reviews.

Balboa Press books may be ordered through booksellers or by contacting:

Balboa Press
A Division of Hay House
1663 Liberty Drive
Bloomington, IN 47403
www.balboapress.com
1-(877) 407-4847

Because of the dynamic nature of the Internet, any Web addresses or links contained in this book may have changed since publication and may no longer be valid. The views expressed in this work are solely those of the author and do not necessarily reflect the views of the publisher, and the publisher hereby disclaims any responsibility for them.

The author of this book does not dispense medical advice or prescribe the use of any technique as a form of treatment for physical, emotional, or medical problems without the advice of a physician, either directly or indirectly. The intent of the author is only to offer information of a general nature to help you in your quest for emotional and spiritual well-being. In the event you use any of the information in this book for yourself, which is your constitutional right, the author and the publisher assume no responsibility for your actions.

Any people depicted in stock imagery provided by Thinkstock are models, and such images are being used for illustrative purposes only. Certain stock imagery © Thinkstock.

ISBN: 978-1-4525-0090-4 (sc)
ISBN 978-1-4525-0092-8 (dj)
ISBN: 978-1-4525-0091-1 (e)

Library of Congress Control Number: 2010918084

Printed in the United States of America

Balboa Press rev. date: 12/7/2010

Dedicated to

My children, Melinda and Andrew, who opened my heart to love
Dorothy Maclean, co-founder of the Findhorn Community
    Way Shower and portal to the beauty of nature
Our Earth Mother, Gaia, and all of the Nature Realm

With love and gratitude to:

Nancy Joy Hefron-my inspiration, my teacher and my number one encourager
Kristi-healer and cherished friend
Minnow-fire soul and kindred spirit
Elisabet-my dear darling friend
Skoti-earth activist and soilmate
Dana-earth healer and friend extraordinaire
Aline-Findhorn friend
Sarah-dimension traveler
Blair-precious to my heart

My wonderful Peace Circle friends, the angels in my life
Karyn-precious to my heart
Heather-soul of an artist, my Celtic connection
Mary Beth-abrazos a mi amiga muy buena
Marlene-wise woman, midwife to soul growth
Roxie-loving heart, gentle soul
Carole-light of courage for the path
Kathy-giving heart, textile art
Teresa-beautiful spirit
Sharon-miracle worker

Come forth into the light of things, let nature be your teacher.

~William Wordsworth

For most of my life, nature was something I took for granted. It was there in the background but not the focus of very much of my time and attention. I would sometimes look at the stars or gaze at a flower or marvel at the river's flow and feel a sense of wonder and amazement. But life was busy and those times were fleeting.

The earth-nature-supplied the air I breathe, the food I eat, the water I drink, my housing, gas for my car and so much more. But it provided so consistently and generously that I didn't stop to think that it is my life support system, the very substance of life itself.

Then, in 2007 our environmental problems finally got my attention in a sobering way. The mind-numbing bad news about destruction of the rain forests, pollution, climate change and myriad other problems really sunk in and I was scared, scared about what the planet would be like for my children and future generations, as well as for us now.

I started doing the recommended things as best I could: more recycling, driving less, writing my members of Congress, joining environmental organizations and talking and obsessing to anyone who would listen about the changes we needed to make.

But as I looked at the magnitude of the problems we faced, my efforts felt inadequate and even futile. I wondered if we, as the human species, had the will and the means to turn things around in time.

I began to wonder if there was something I was missing, answers in places that I hadn't looked. Einstein said that 'we can't solve problems by using the same kind of thinking we used when we created them.' So, perhaps our problems were really an invitation, an opportunity to find a better way to live as we found ways to clean up the mess we created.

I was drawn to the education center and spiritual community at Findhorn, Scotland and participated in a life-changing workshop called "Connecting to God and Nature". It was led by Dorothy Maclean who was a pioneer in communication with the nature realm. As I learned and talked to Dorothy and others there, I felt like I had come home. I realized that there was so much more to nature than meets the eye. I learned and remembered what the indigenous people have always known-that nature is alive with spirit and indwelling life.

Since then, my life has changed and expanded in miraculous and beautiful ways. I feel connected to nature and the earth in ways I never could have imagined. I have discovered that indeed there is more to the world of nature than our physical eyes can see or our minds can comprehend. I have found the beauty and spirit of nature that only our hearts can feel and discern. In the process, I have met and connected to other people who love the earth and are passionate about restoring it to health. They are gifts and I cherish our friendship and mutual support.

I have come to believe that the answers to our environmental problems are part of our search for peace, contentment and connection to spirit. Nature is not something for humans to dominate or control. It truly can be our teacher, our partner, our friend and our path out of the mess we have created through our overconsumption of resources and 'looking for love in all the wrong places'.

Humans have a very important role to play as we seek to restore the earth to health. But we don't have to do it alone. Nature is resilient and alive with healing power. We are a part of nature and can learn to create abundance, just as nature does. As we connect to nature and join with other people, we can find fulfillment that will heal our spirits and heal the earth.

The messages and writings in this book are my attempt to share the gifts I have been given. I hope that the joy and peace that I have found will touch your life, as well. My wish for you is that you will feel the love that is so abundantly available to us from the nature realm-only love, always love, love overflowing.

Blessings,

Mary Kirkpatrick

Meditation on being Keepers of the Earth:

Remember.

Remember a time when people lived in harmony with nature and each other.

Fighting and war were not.

We lived in keeping with the heartbeat of the earth's rhythms.

Close your eyes, breathe and remember.

We cannot go back but listen. Is it not a siren's call? A quiet voice emerging from the deep places in our soul?

It urges us to be still, listen, sit a while in wonder of the miracles that surround us.

For a moment, leave behind the striving, the noise, the material things that consume our time and thoughts.

See our world transformed. The excrement of our tailpipes and smokestacks no longer suffocates our trees, our fields, our earth, us. The sounds of chainsaws and motors are silenced.

Remember. How long have we been given all we need-air to breathe, cold water to quench our thirst, food to nourish us and shelter from the cold? How long have we taken, mindless of the precious gifts?

What have we given back?

Feel the grief hidden in our hearts. The searching and needing and longing to find quiet places inside of us and out.

Listen to the wind and the happy sound of water in a brook. Hear the cheerful birds and marvel at the beauty always near.

And when we hear and see and feel, how do we respond?

Is it not time to say yes to God, to ourselves, to our earth and no to what can never satisfy us? Is it not time to heed the message of scientists who warn of ecological disaster if we continue to destroy our earth, the balance of our air and land and water and living things?

If we don't listen and remember, who will inherit the legacy? Is it not our children and grandchildren not yet born?

When our great grandchildren say, remember, do we not want them to remember our courage, our ingenuity and our passion to leave the earth better than we found it?

We could do it out of fear. But let us do it out of love, for self, for Creator and all of creation.

Who can imagine the blessings and gifts of our choices?

A butterfly emerging from the chrysalis into a world on a path to health.

A child free of fear from a world damaged by our current choices.

Us, peaceful and living in harmony with each other and our earthly home.

Laughter in tinkling brooks, ocean waves, a piece of sky, a green meadow calling for a playmate.

Remember, then join together to make a new memory.

Let us begin now.

> *But I know every rock and tree and creature*
> *Has a life, has a spirit, has a name.*
>
> **~From the Disney movie Pocahontas**

At the 'Connecting to God and Nature' workshop I took at Findhorn, Scotland, I learned that many cultures have long believed that there is part of the angel realm that is connected to nature. The devas are the architects that make the templates, blueprints and plans for nature's creations. The nature spirits, sometimes called elementals, are the ones who turn energy into form so we have the parts of nature that our eyes can see-trees, flowers, rocks, rain and so forth.

This has enriched my view of nature beyond description. I used to look at a tree or plant and just see a 'thing', the physical form of a tree or other plant. Now I see so much more, when I look with my heart, as well as my eyes. I see beautiful life forms and also nature beings that are my friends. We, humans, are part of nature! What nature does for plants and animals, it does for us, too. It provides our food which becomes our bodies. It gives us all we need for life, so many gifts and blessings.

The part of nature that I first connected to and received messages from was Gaia, the deva of our planet earth, the Goddess. She truly is our Earth Mother, loving and strong, heart and arms outstretched to share her love with us.

I also connected to Pan, god of the woodlands who, as one author says, is the CEO of the nature spirits, full of power and also love. Other messages are from the devas of particular plants or parts of nature. Some I was inspired to write to or about nature.

Mary Kirkpatrick

Messages from Gaia

This is the first message I received from Gaia:

The Goddess is rising. Long has she waited to take her rightful place beside the male. She does not seek to dominate or control the male but to be a partner, to co-create a new heaven and a new earth.

Now is the time! Can you not sense the birthing, the joy? The contractions are closer together now. The new is ready to be born.

The Goddess, Gaia, rejoices to find those who are vanguards of the new order, people who respect and reverence the female and celebrate her beauty and mystery. Gaia smiles her happiness and gratitude to each of you who are a part of this. In this space, women can release the pain of the past and find the loveliness of this new way of living.

Long has the male dominated and destroyed the essence of the female. Rape, terror, molestation, shame and harshness. These are the legacy of millennia of male abuse of power.

Women carry the pain, this ancient pain in their bodies, their minds, their souls. It is imbedded in their cellular memory and it haunts their every moment. They carry the memory of women forced to live in slavery, used for male pleasure and when nothing else could control them, burned at the stake, stripped of their dignity, beaten and tortured, their gentle nature destroyed by this treatment.

Men carry the burden of shame for what has been done by generations before them, stretching back for countless centuries. Women's loss has not been their gain for all have been diminished by this madness. Men ache for this ugliness, repulsed and horrified by this inheritance.

A cleansing flood is washing away the past, releasing us from its bondage. Can you not feel the freedom rising from the depths of the earth? Is not the Goddess Gaia, Mother Earth, lifting her hands in gladness, joined by the Great Spirit, Father Sky as He joins her in glorious celebration.

We are a part of it! We are witnesses and celebrants in this awakening, this birthing. With joy and gratitude we lift up our hearts and minds and yea, our very souls, unable to contain the heartfelt joy we feel.

The butterfly is emerging from the chrysalis, its moist wings ready to carry the new life in flight. The sun and moon are converging in a resonance, a rhythm that cannot be denied or halted. The earth is singing a new song of glorious celebration for this transformation.

Let us join in the music, the dancing, the release of pent-up expectation turned into radiant reality. Let us become the mystery, the majesty, the partners in this co-creation.

Oh, Gaia, Goddess, friend, female. Oh Great Spirit, Creator, male. We lift our hands and our voices in a joyful shout. We offer our humble thanks and consecrate this moment to your honor. We take what we have shared here with us into the world, ready to do our part to carry this message to every corner of the earth.

September 9, 2008

From the rubble and the ashes, the Goddess rises.
Do you see fire and destruction?
Yes, but look again.
The old must disappear for the new to be born.
The earth is in labor now, pushing and contracting.
Have you seen birth? Have you participated in it?
It's a mess!
The egg cracks, the membrane ruptures and the amniotic fluid gushes.
There's blood and pain and a cry for help.

But feel the exultation, the joy, the freedom, the excitement.
New life, wings where they were not before.
Look around you, see up ahead.
See the majesty, the mystery, the miracles revealed.
Most see death, endings, the familiar and comfortable fading away.
And they are afraid as they cling to what exists but soon will be no more.

A precious few can see the new and they are precious indeed.
They hold the hand of the Goddess as the earth heaves and contracts and pushes the new life forms through the birth canal into the radiant future.
She is not afraid, neither should we be.
She exists in a place beyond time and calls us there, to her heart, where love is all there is,
nothing else; only, always love.

This is not random, it's no coincidence that we are here now, in this place, with plans and dreams that shatter the old order and will help to create the new.
Be glad! Enjoy it all! Every bit!
The Goddess holds out her hand, yes, her heart, as well.
Be still a moment. Feel the beat, the rhythm, the sacred breath.

Reach out, open your hands and your heart
The gifts are yours, freely given.
Take them and celebrate the wonder, the miracles, the magic.
She's smiling out to you.
Love is flowing, gushing, flooding from her heart to yours.
Let it wash over you, refresh you, fill you.

The Goddess is teacher, companion, friend.
So are you. Yes, you!
She could create the new but she wants us to be a part of it.
Co-creator, co-creation.
It's a gift beyond price, of value that cannot be measured in the seen world, only in the unseen.

Ask for what you need.
It will be given in abundance, beyond your wildest expectations.
Your hands cannot hold it all so share and all will be blessed.
The contractions will subside, the new will shine in all its splendor.
And you will know in your heart that it is yours.

Goddess Rising!
October 23, 2008

Feel the hush. It's hard to breathe as the reality of the impending birth sinks into my heart, my soul.

The womb, place of the gestation of new life, is now empty. The new life form is in the birth canal, is birthing, being pushed out, entering the earth…reaching, stretching rejoicing to bring the new, be the new.

One more push and the new is born, enters our world, joins our world, becomes our world and we are one.

Breathe…breathe…breathe

Feel the quiet excitement, the joy, the celebration. It's happened! The new is here. The separation is healed!!

Who knew. We thought this day, this time was far away in the distant future. Many never sensed it as even a possibility. But now, now, yes NOW, it is reality!

Surely some intuitively knew it was possible, even sensed its approach. But now? Us? Here?? Surely, that's impossible, too good to be true.

But we're not ready. The earth is a mess. The timing must be off, the birth premature.

No. My dear children, beloved ones, precious partners, my dear darling co-creators.

How is the new birthed? Do plants emerge in their mature form? Are animals and people birthed in their adult stage?

No! The seed is small, babies fragile. They are new and fresh, perfect bearers of the new. And I, the One who births, I know the timing. It's now! Let's dance and celebrate, rejoice!

Be happy. Look around you. The old order is collapsing. It has outlived its usefulness. Let it go. A fire is spreading across the earth, the old is dying, the new is being born. Know for sure that the Goddess is rising.

What is the new? You need only look within your heart to see.

Harmony-all creation attuned and held in the same energy.

Peace-inside and out, no more striving and fruitless searching. The new, before unseen, is now visible. Touch it and know that it is true.

Love-truly all is contained in this pervasive, all-encompassing love. Always love, only love, nothing else. The illusions are vanishing. Let them disappear.

All you need will be provided. All wisdom, all love, all gifts-they are already along the path you will take. Just walk with open hands and open hearts and they will appear. Feel the joy of this discovery.

As the Goddess rises, so does love. Separateness is no more.

Take my hand, beloved ones, and each others hands. From the dust of stars we will create beauty together, always together. The broken will be healed, the web of life restored to glorious perfection. The broken will be joined in wonderful wholeness. Nature will be beautiful beyond our wildest imagination.

Breathe in the truth of this loveliness. Be peaceful amidst the storms. Know that all is well, that this birthing is a time of great joy.

Rest against the bosom of the Goddess for she is love, tender and gentle. Join the rhythm of her quietly beating heart. Time slips away as this stillness brings all into a oneness that cannot be divided.

You are loved. Indeed you are love. Love overflowing. The Goddess, the Mother loves you. Rest in this. Breathe it into your heart.

I love you, says the Goddess. We are one.

Written on Election night when Barack Obama was elected President of the United States

Goddess Rising
November 4, 2008

Surely on this historic night, doubt is fading. Surely you must sense that the Goddess is rising.

The birth is behind us. Have you seen a birthing? The Mother's position is vulnerable, precarious. All of her energy is focused on safely pushing the new life into the world. She is at risk and needs protection.

The Goddess is no longer in the birthing position. She holds the new life, indeed all of life, in her arms of love. She is strong, yet gentle. Determined, yet tender. Full of resolve, yet also quiet and peaceful.

A new energy is rising on the earth. Division and separation are giving way to oneness, wholeness. Fear is losing its stronghold-powerless against the tidal wave of love that no barrier can contain. Just as darkness vanishes when light appears, so it is when Gaia's heart love overflows and sends its healing touch to every corner of the earth and beyond.

This is a time of rejoicing and gladness. This is the turning time when we must leave behind the past and embrace the new.

The winds of change now whisper, heard by only those who are quiet and have grown to a place where this voice can be heard. Each day more join the new, ready to share its wonder and joy.

My voice will be clearer as time unfolds. Soon all will know that the Goddess is rising. My arms are reaching out, full of gifts freely offered. Open your hands! Open your heart to receive them!

It's only one gift really. It's love rising from the earth and descending from the heavens, converging at this place, at this time, to seed the transformation and move the unseen to the seen.

You are a part of it, my beloved ones! Long have I waited for this moment, as we create the future together with shared love and a shared heart. Hear the music. Join the dancing! Run into my arms and snuggle close. A home is waiting here for you, my precious ones.

Don't be distracted by the chaos and problems of the world. I am well able to care for my dear children. But I need your help! I need your hands to heal, your words to teach, your hearts to love and your steps to lead the way for others to follow.

All you need is here for you. Rest in me and you will find peace. Come into my arms of love and find contentment. Let's share a smile and sing a happy song.

The clouds will disappear and the warm and cheerful sun will bring joy to you. The nature spirits have already joined us and share the path. Welcome them and miracles will amaze and delight you.

Know that I care tenderly for you in each moment of your waking and sleeping. The Goddess loves you. Yes, you are her precious ones, her beloved.

I love you, says the Goddess. We are one.

Goddess Rising
November 8, 2008

My children, beloved ones,

How I love you! It is my joy to reach out to you, dear ones.

This is a time of great change for the earth and indeed for realms, seen and unseen. Don't be confused or dismayed. All is well. I hold you close to my heart where you are safe, protected.

You see problems all around you. I could change things in the twinkling of an eye. But how could I choose to dis-empower you in that way?

Look around you. Solutions and answers are sprinkled everywhere. What are problems? Are they not opportunities to grow and learn?

You are strong and resilient, intelligent and wise. Yet you need each other. Be like the oak trees who entwine their roots with each other. Even a strong wind, yea a mighty storm, cannot destroy them for together they can withstand the strongest gale.

Put your heads together. Perhaps the way to healing is like a puzzle. I give each person a part and together you will discover wonders and mysteries to satisfy your souls.

You cannot see the path to the future? It cannot be seen with your eyes for your eyes only see the physical.

Look with your heart. Close your eyes. Put your hands over your heart and breathe. Feel my peace wash over you. Listen, my precious ones. My messages come softly, gently. Your heart knows, it will lead the way.

This is the turning time and the progress and changes are well underway. The cold winter winds cannot stop what is happening. The seeds are sprouting and new life is pushing its way toward the light. It is emerging, bursting forth in joy to greet the new day. Welcome it with open arms and open hearts!

Do you still have doubts? Do you think the problems are too big, the changes too slow? That's good! Then look in new places for the help you need. Can you see the Goddess rising? Perhaps there is more you can't see! Of course there is!! You are surrounded by beings who love you and are waiting expectantly, prepared and very much ready to help you, to accomplish all that is needed. They are not limited as you are. Hmm, are you bound by limits? Ask and see, my beloved ones. It is my delight to surprise you with gifts of beauty and miracles.

You are seeds, dear ones! You hold all you need in your hearts. New life is bubbling to the surface. It is glorious! Close your eyes and breathe the beauty into your heart.

All you need will be provided. You are my partners, my chosen ones, opening doors so others can follow and find the new. All is on schedule. The old is disappearing, vanishing like the darkness when light comes. You are creating the new and no words can adequately describe the joy you will find as you emerge from the chrysalis and find that a new world awaits.

Tend the land. Care for each other. Welcome the new with open hearts. I hold you tenderly against my heart. Indeed we share the same heart. I am the Goddess, Gaia, and we are one.

From the Goddess, Gaia
December 7, 2008

Dear ones, beloved and precious to my heart of hearts,

These messages come to you in intervals but my love for you and my communication with you is constant, like a river's flow. The Source is eternal, infinite, miraculous.

The Source is a Heart, your Mother's Heart and your Father's Heart. Remember that you are partners, not helpless children. You are children, but now you are grown children-mature adults who are fully prepared to co-create and return the earth to paradise.

The time is now! All is ready! You can feel this truth if you but close your eyes, open your heart and breathe the breath of life that encompasses all. Do that now, dear ones. Close your eyes and breathe, breathe, breathe. You will feel my presence as a mighty force, everywhere, always.

It is not outside of you. It is inside of you, infilling and indwelling within you. Smile! Be joyful, my darling and beloved children. All is well. All is held in my tender care.

Look around you. Do you see massive, intractable problems? They are gifts. Know that each problem is an opportunity and the solution is built into it, fully available to you, to humanity. It's like a riddle, a puzzle. Study it and the solution will be clear, obvious.

As you solve the problems and dilemmas, you will move forward and the future is glorious, filled with beauty beyond your ability to fully comprehend. So rejoice, right now, this very instant! Open your arms, your hands, your hearts, for I can't wait to fill them with priceless gifts of restoration and perfection.

Don't be gloomy. Take time to laugh in joy with me. Dance with me. Delight with me. The good things are not elusive, planted only in the future. They are here NOW, accessible to you at all times, if you but accept them.

I love you! I am not waiting until you improve. You are perfection in my eyes now! I love you now! I always have and I always and forever will. Come close, come very near. Put your arms around me and I will draw you into a tender, intimate embrace. Breathe and you will feel my heart, beating in a gentle rhythm. Breathe and you will sense your heart, joined with mine, beating with mine. We are one, my beloved ones. You are one with me and one with each other. Take each others hands, my sweet earthlings. ☺ You will know the joy that banishes all loneliness or sense of separation.

The illusion of separateness is being healed now. It will vanish as the sun dispels the morning dew. All that is left is beauty, love everywhere, kisses and hugs for all. The music of the universe resonates in your souls, a lovely tune of joyfulness and peace. Each of you is a note in the song, the whole. Each of you is a ray of the light. Each of you is a vital part of the flow of love and life.

I love you, my precious ones. I never leave you. I am love. I am buckets of love, showers of love, torrents of love, rainbows of love. Breathe it into your heart, your souls and you will know peace that can never be shaken. My love is freely and bountifully offered to you, love overflowing.

I am Gaia, your Earth Mother, your friend

From the Goddess:
December 12, 2008

Beloved ones, dear and precious to my heart,

What do I want to say to you this morning? It is this: Ask! Ask! Ask! Yes! ASK! That is such an important message for you to grasp. You need to stretch your minds and then stretch them some more so you can begin to more fully understand how incredibly important your thoughts are.

First of all, ask yourselves why your thoughts are so important. What is your answer? Then consider this. Your thoughts create reality, they create the future, they create now. (they created the past, too-now do you more fully understand their importance?) Do you realize that when you think something that aligns with my thoughts, it is instantly created in the Unseen realm?? Yes! It becomes an energy form. It is real from that time forward. You co-created it! That's why your thoughts are vital to this Turning Time.

When the time is right, the energy form that is co-created because of your thoughts, joined with the Divine, becomes a physical form. But always remember that the creation began with your thoughts, your divine ability to conceive of it. You are one with the Unseen, the Divine.

I know that this is perhaps challenging for you to grasp. It is expansive and miraculous. And I hope you find it beautiful, my precious and beloved children and partners. It is such beauty to me, such joy to share myself with you in this loveliness of creation. Always humans have had this capacity. But it was buried, unrecognized, untapped.

Now! Now! Now!!! Now is the birthing, the invisible coming into sight. It happens in two ways. One way is that the Divine turns energy into form so you can see it. The other part is that your eyes develop their ability to see more than they used to be able to see. The portals between the Seen and Unseen burst open and all becomes one, whole and visible to those with eyes to see and hearts to accept and arms to embrace.

Come near until our Hearts are one, beating with the same rhythm. Come close and dance the dance of life with me. Rejoice and be glad for heaven is streaming to earth until those boundaries fade and disappear and all that remains is love, only love, always love, love overflowing.

YOU are part of the flow. Just breathe the breath of life with Me and know that all is happening as it needs to. Think big, expansive thoughts and dream dreams of beauty, growth and perfection. They will come to pass, even now they are in the womb of creation, thanks to you and your beauty. Your breaths are the birthing contractions, bringing beauty into form. Thank you, dear ones, for I need you more than you can imagine. My essence is creation but to co-create with you is joy beyond what words can describe.

Be love, breathe love. Then ask and your dreams will appear. Miracles await you, very much ready to be born. You are a part of the flow, you are the flow. I hold you in arms of love, so near to my heart that we are one, indeed. I love you, dear ones. We are one.

I am Gaia, your Earth Mother, your friend

From Gaia
December 18, 2008

Dear ones, beloved and precious to my heart,

I draw you close to my heart, comforted by our oneness, knowing that we are all a part of the whole. What do I mean by that? Consider the ocean. Each drop of water is separate, distinct. Yet all are part of the ocean. I am Gaia, I am the ocean. You are the drops of water, you are part of me and I am you. Is that not joy indeed? It is to me! You are together, as well, my darlings. Just as drops of water are bound together, so are you part of the whole and each other. You are never, ever alone. You have me and you have each other. All is well.

Consider the leaves on a tree. Each is a part of the tree, of the whole. Together they are one life. In a play there are many characters but they are all part of the same story. As you recognize this truth, you will be blessed with friendship, love and peace.

This is a time of great contrasts. There is great upheaval in and on the earth and change in the Unseen realms, the energy fields. There are deaths and endings and people are grieving and sad and frightened. But there are birthings, new life being formed, new ways of living are coming into being. Imbedded in the new is joy, light and great rejoicing. Reach out for the new and it is yours.

This is the chrysalis time. The caterpillar had its time, its place. It was a precious life form. But now is the time of transformation. It is time for all to find their wings and fly!

Each of you has a part in this birthing process. Others can help to create the space, the place for birth. But each must do their part to create the new. I could do it for you. But then you would be passive, not partners. I want to share all with you. I love you dearly and am blessed as you grow and join in glad co-creation with me.

There are myriad Helpers in all times and places. Ask! Ask! Ask! Your friends and partners in the nature realm are waiting for you to acknowledge them and ask for their help. They have powers and abilities that are beyond your current capacity to understand. But ask anyway! Some things cannot happen unless you ask. Ask for big, miraculous things and you will be amazed and thrilled to see what we can accomplish together. What is impossible for you can happen in the twinkling of an eye when you ask for help. Try and see. I will hold you in my arms of love through it all and that is joy beyond description.

Current methods and ways of doing things cannot solve the problems the earth now faces. That's good news! It means you must seek and find new ways which will bring in the New. The old will vanish as darkness disappears when light comes. The new will be glorious, filled with love, peace and gentle wonder.

Rest in my arms when you are weary. I will whisper words of love and comfort and we will be one. Stay close to me and watch as the new comes into form.

I love you, my dear ones. Breathe in the love that is ever near to you. Lean against me and listen to my heart, become part of my heart.

I love you, darlings. I am Gaia, your Earth Mother, your friend

From Gaia
December 27, 2008

Dear Ones, beloved and precious to my heart,

The old year is ending, the new is birthing. Look around you and listen, feel the rhythms of the earth. Now is a time of quietness and stillness. The bear slumbers, the seed sleeps.

Take time to embrace this resting time. Breathe deeply of the silence and the peacefulness all around you.

Yes, there is chaos and disturbance on the earth. Have you seen a chicken when its head has been cut off? It is no longer living but it thrashes about and can leave damage in its path. Let things be, this will pass.

The physical forms of the earth and on the earth cannot remain. The physical is a reflection of what is happening in the unseen realm, the unseen world. The energy there has changed, is changing even now. Celebrate! As the old vanishes, it creates space for the new and it will be glorious!!

I want you to ask, ask ask! But know that your minds cannot wrap themselves around what is being born. Don't be surprised when I give you more than you could even imagine asking for! Yet, it's important that you ask, for in so doing you stretch your mind to envision new thoughts and forms. You create portals, openings for them to enter the earth realm.

What you think and do and feel is important!! We are in a time of co-creation and you are an active part of that.

The old forms and ways of living have served their purpose. They were needed in their time. But now is the time for rebirth and change. Old institutions are crumbling, outdated and ineffective in the new energy. Let them go. They had strengths but they were also filled with injustices, inequities and abuse.

The new is a higher order. Connection instead of separateness. Peace, not conflict. Wholeness where before there was dividedness. People are clinging to the old because they don't understand the beauty that lies ahead.

You are the bridge. You see what is possible and can teach and lead others. Take their hands and walk with them when they are ready. Be a light. When they see your joy, they will find hope for the future.

Take each other's hands, as well. Feel the friendship and warmth of caring companions to share the journey into the new. Know for sure that you are never, ever alone. I send all you need. I hold out my arms and welcome you close. Rest against my heart and breathe in love. You will find peace and a gentle contentment. Close your eyes and all will be revealed. It is just a heartbeat away, my darlings.

I love you, dear ones. My love overflows, washing over you like a refreshing shower. You are held in arms of love, my arms, each other's arms.

I am Gaia, your Earth Mother, your friend

From Gaia
January 20, 2009

Dear Ones, beloved and cherished,

Tonight I come softly, gently, quietly. What a relief it is to find those who are still and able to hear my whisper. Thank you, dear ones, for what you give to me. It is my joy, my song.

With so many people, I have to raise my voice to be heard above the noise. How I long for quiet times when we can speak to each other in peace and gladness, unburdened by the loudness that wears at the soul.

I yearn for my precious ones to feel the love I pour out, never ceasing. Love is everywhere, always! It swirls about in a dance of love, touching all. Yet the hearts of so many of my people are closed, walled off. They think it is protection but it blocks the love that is ever near.

Now is the new, the turning time! Yes! Things may not look new but they are being transformed from the inside. The changes can be seen clearly by those with eyes attuned to the Spirit realm and ears that hear the melodies of Earth and nature.

This is a time of deep and profound healing. My people are doubled over in pain, yet many are unaware of it. Problems are like the scalpel that lances the wound and clears the way for healing. The pain need only last an instant. I open my arms wide and rejoice when my precious ones run into my embrace and let me touch the hurting places with the sure promise of all things restored to health and wholeness.

I need you, my partners in co-creation! Indeed you are the keys that unlock the doors to mystery and wonder. Believe it! Breathe and give this time half a chance for that is all that is needed for miracles that make all things new. Your faith is like the sun that dispels the dew and causes the fog to disappear, revealing the beauty that was always there.

It is not complicated. It is as simple as a smile that cheers a person filled with sadness. It is a warm touch that gladdens someone burdened by fear and dread.

Extend that smile and that touch to all. Never doubt that a tree is strengthened by your admiring glance or a friendly squirrel uplifted by your tender thought. The birds thrive when you notice them and even the soil sighs with happiness when you send a bit of gentle gratitude its way.

If you have questions, ask and I will share my wisdom and reveal my truths. Do you need help, assistance, anything at all? Ask! Tell me what you need. I'll listen to every word and send gifts in rich abundance.

Are you tired? Come to me for rest. Are you weary? Bring me your burdens and I'll carry them for you. Are you lonely? Reach out your hands. I'll send friends and kindred spirits to share the path.

And I will share the path with you, every step! I'll take your hand and restore your strength. We'll stop a moment and I will draw you into my arms for a cozy snuggle. What is time when our hearts are near, beating in a soothing rhythm that sends its healing power into the living ether, cleansing and refreshing all it touches. Time and cares will slip away as we share this intimate and timeless moment. Rest your head upon my shoulder and breathe the breath of life with me. We are one with all and with each other.

I love you, dear ones. You are precious to my heart. Be of good courage. You are a part of this chrysalis time, very much helping me to co-create beauty and transformation in the Seen and Unseen realms.

I love you now and always. I am Gaia, your Earth Mother, your friend.

From Gaia
February 20, 2009

My darlings, beloved and dear to my heart,

Good morning! How I love to greet you each and every day!!

My love is like the rain that falls gently from the sky, touching every inch of earth. The only thing that prevents it from hitting any given spot is human created barriers. The rain is there, just as my love is! Stand in a place where it can fall upon you in joyful abandon. Raise your face to the sky! Open your hands, your heart, your arms and embrace each precious drop!

My love is like the ocean, massive and expansive. (Actually my love is much larger than the ocean but you get the picture ☺) My love is deep and wide and all-encompassing. You are the channel, the riverbed for love's flow. YOU are the ones who decide how much love can reach you. Do you provide a streambed? Then you shall receive a happy stream of love from me!

But ask yourself: do I want only a stream of love? Or, do I want a river of love, flowing, from Gaia's heart to mine? And, how big the river, dear ones? A small river or one that is really big-perhaps the Amazon? Oh, please, please, please! Give me a really big riverbed and see what happens!

My love is unlimited! Please, stretch your mind to believe this. Expand your heart to accept love's flow. I want to flood you with love so very much. As you open the floodgates of your heart, be ready for miracles to occur in an ever expanding crescendo!

Close your eyes and breath the breath of life. Deep inside your heart, do you not find a knowing that things are shifting and changing? Indeed the earth's energy is changing and vibrating at an increasingly faster vibration.

Some people are unaware on a conscious level and try to ignore the changes they are sensing. They rush about, busy with the mundane, daily tasks of living. They are fearful and apprehensive.

Others are more aware of the changes and are actively resisting. It's pointless, really, but they are too afraid to consider the joyous truth. They create a dam but it will only serve to increase the flood when the dam breaks. And that is good! For the flood will bring beauty that no one can fully comprehend or imagine. So, thank them for their gift, even when it appears to be disastrous.

But you, my darling children, you are light and love. You know that you are made of the same molecules that form the stars! You are strength and peace and love. Claim your birthright! Stand tall and be glad. Nothing can stop the glorious future from arriving and it will be here very soon, more quickly than you can imagine. Perhaps it is as close as your next breath, the next beat of your heart.

Here is your choice: walk along the river using your own effort OR jump into the river and let it carry you along. I am the river's flow. You are a glorious part of me. I am so very willing and most anxious to have you be the river with me.

We are one, dear ones. I love you with a love overflowing and majestic. I hold you so close to my heart and never, ever leave you. I cradle you tenderly in my bosom where you are safe and warm. You need never leave this place of love for I cherish our togetherness more than you can imagine.

I love you, dear ones. I am Gaia, your Earth Mother, your friend

From Gaia
March 27, 2009

My darlings, beloved of my heart,

Surely, in this springtime of growth and light, you can sense for sure that the Goddess is rising!

Feel the earth pulsing with excitement. I love spring, too! The winter is my quiet time, soft and silent. Now the energy is rising and I am rejoicing to share it with your eyes and your hearts.

I know there is destruction all around. Yes, it hurts but never forget that I have a Mother's heart. Does not a Mother give of herself to her beloved ones? Of course! The earth is teacher and selfless giver. I make visible the damage and pain that is in your hearts. For who would hurt the earth, save those that are sad, lonely and frightened?

Know that all is well. I have strength and myriad helpers in the Unseen realm! I am simply waiting for people to awaken from their stupor and blindness and co-create with me, returning the earth to Paradise. And, yeah, it is more than that. It is truly a new birthing, not a return to the past. We are making all things new!

Dance with me! Look into my eyes and see the love, flowing in wild abandon from a never ending Source! Come into my arms of love and snuggle close, warmed and blessed by our togetherness. How I love our times together! I love you, my precious ones, always and forever.

So many are unseeing. Is it any wonder that I dance with joy when you come near? I love to feel your fingers in the earth. It is shared joy, my dear ones. I feel your love when you look upon the earth, the soil, the stones, the plants and little creatures. I breathe it in and feel our oneness that can never be divided or shaken.

Breathe love, be love. Step forward in quiet confidence, knowing that you are surrounded by the devas and nature spirits-your partners in co-creation. I am always near, helping and guiding. So is Pan, the one who turns energy into form. You are a vital and incredibly important part of this! It is your thoughts that create the template for visible form!!

Dream big, audacious dreams!! Picture them in clear details! Then ask! Ask, ask, ask!!! Keep asking. You cannot comprehend how important it is that you ask!!! Some things cannot become Seen unless you ask! How it delights my Mother's heart to have you ask for what you want and need and can imagine!! The devas and nature spirits swirl near, most capable of turning your dreams into reality!! Their essence is joy and light and music. They are perfection but they need you! You are co-creators, that is your gift and my gift to you.

Take quiet moments to spend time with me for I am most happy to share all that I have and all that I am. I adore you, my darlings! I am ever near, always glad to share hugs and gentle kisses upon your cheeks. I brush you softly with the wind and send a bird's song to cheer your heart. I send love to you, love overflowing.

I love you, precious ones.

I am Gaia, your Earth Mother, your friend

From Gaia
May 01, 2009

Dear ones, beloved of my heart,

The energy is rising, surely and certainly. Those who predict the future based on the past are going to face surprises and, for some, a rude awakening.

The old order is collapsing to make way for the new. Some find this to be frightening, others are angry or dismayed.

To you I say, rejoice!! Be glad and celebrate. The old ways were filled with bondage and injustice. The new is freedom and abundance. Which will you choose?

I whisper, choose newness! Indeed I shout it in joyful abandon. I want to share it with <u>you</u>, my darlings! It is a gift, freely given. Open your hands and your hearts and it is yours, now and forever.

Don't look back. A glance is okay-to get your bearings and to remember where you have come from. But focus on today, with all its opportunities and miracles and love overflowing.

All is well. Never doubt that all is happening with exquisite timing and unfolding beauty. You are loved beyond measure, held gently and tenderly in a warm embrace. Snuggle close and you can feel my breath, the rhythmic beating of my heart. Rest here when you are weary from the world's cares. Here you can find peace, contentment, fulfillment and rest for your soul.

Drink of the water that flows from an unending Source. Dance and sing, for the melody is for you, dear ones.

Don't cling to the old ways, for they are collapsing and disintegrating and soon will be no more. Instead watch expectantly for the new to appear, moving from the Unseen to the Seen. Welcome the new for it is glorious and transforming.

If you need to cling to something, cling to me for I am love, only love, always love, love without end or boundary.

The new is emerging in loveliness and enticing fragrance. It is here even now! Just breathe and sense it in your heart, emerging like a butterfly from the chrysalis.

I love you, my precious ones. I am Gaia, your Earth Mother, your friend.

From Gaia
July 2, 2009

My darlings, beloved and precious,

Is more becoming clear to you all the time? Can you now see that the New is here? Yes! New ways of living and being are here NOW, today, this instant!! Joy, peace, love-all are as close as your next thought, your next breath, the next beat of your heart that joins with my heart to co-create all.

Yes, it is co-creation indeed! I supply the paint and the canvas. But you are the artists, creating beauty in your gardens and in your lives. I supply the music and you dance the dance of life with me and my nature beings! I give the tools and the seeds and the soil. You plant the seeds and sprinkle water on them and see what we create together! The plants fairly wriggle with delight to share space with you!! The birds and little creatures of the earth draw near to you, so thrilled to share energy and time with you!

All is well!! Truly!!! I exist in a place beyond time, beyond the physical. I can communicate and move between realms and boundaries and dimensions. In the twinkling of an eye, I could change all. But that would not be fun for me. I would miss the joy of sharing all with you. You have the ability to create all with me. Come! Take my hand and I will reveal everything to you! I love you so much, dear ones!

The problems you see are but portals, doors, pathways to the new. They are invitations to rise to a new place, to claim your power to co-create and change all to beauty and love. This is a time of love, only love, always love, love overflowing. There is an ocean of love surrounding you, now and always and forever. The only questions are: Can you see love? Are you willing to access love? How much will you take? Will you hold out a small cup and take that much? Or will you open your arms, take a deep breath and plunge into it, trusting that you will float and fly?

Love is buoyant and expansive. It is carrying all into the New. The old ways and forms are disappearing. The new are being birthed. All is well and on time. Please-take my hand and look into my eyes. Come close to me, heart to heart, and you will feel love, share love, know love. I respond to the smallest bit of willingness, the quietest whisper of need.

Take each other's hands. Now is the time of community, of sharing the joy and excitement of entering the new spaces. You will learn together, discover together, find joy together. None are meant to be alone. We will be together and it will be glorious indeed.

I love you, my darlings. I am Gaia, your Earth Mother, your friend

From Gaia
September 15, 2009

Dear ones, beloved to my heart,

Can you feel the energy shifting and strengthening? Indeed the Earth is entering a new phase and humanity, as well. There can be no doubt that the Goddess is rising.

Some are unaware, thinking that things will continue as they have in the past. Others sense the shifts and are frightened.

Ah, but you, dear ones, are tuned in to what is happening. You are my Light Bearers, my Way Showers. You are like a beacon on a hill, like a lighthouse, showing others the way to the new shore.

Old ways are vanishing, the new is being born. The question for you is: how will you enter the new? Think of the life stages of mariposa-egg, caterpillar and then the beauty of the butterfly after the chrysalis time has ended. In this new era, you will need your wings! Indeed there may be trouble ahead for those who are still crawling around in their caterpillar stage. They cannot take flight and rise above chaos of the transition that is underway.

My precious ones, all is well. This is a time of great joy and transformation. Spread your wings and take flight. You will see the changes that are occurring from an expansive perspective. Stay peaceful and you can soar! Don't get caught up in the chaos and confusion of this chrysalis time. Don't cling to the old for the new is beautiful beyond comprehension.

Remember the story of Beauty and the Beast. When love reached a critical mass, the old bondage dissipated and all were able to see and experience the perfection that was always there, simply invisible and unreachable for a time. Be watchful for this is very much the template for the new heaven and the new earth.

Rest against my heart, dear ones. Come close for a cozy snuggle. Then reach out to others who are walking the path that you are. You will find a deep contentment that will satisfy the longing of your soul.

I love you, my darlings. I am Gaia, your Earth Mother, your friend.

From Gaia
September 24, 2009

My darling and precious children, beloved ones,

This message comes to you wrapped in love, only love, always love, love overflowing. Indeed, that is the theme of this Transformation Time. Love is streaming from the heavens and rising from the earth. It surrounds you like a warm and comforting cloud, a blanket of strong, yet gentle love. Breathe it into your heart and snuggle into its cozy hug.

Quiet your mind and heart and find that still place deep inside you, where the cares of the world cannot touch. Here you can access the oneness of all Creation. In this place, perfection dwells. You are a part of it! Yes!! YOU are perfection! Oh, my precious ones, I see only perfection when I look at you. I see your essence, your radiant being and it is beautiful beyond description.

I want so very much for you to see your perfection, as well. It is like opening a present and seeing loveliness under the wrapping. That is what I see when I look at you with my heart. Look within and you will see it, too. I promise!! Then, let us dance with joy! Celebrate and be glad with me, my darlings.

I offer this gift to all but so many are unable to see. Their eyes are closed. They are hiding behind walls and are unaware of what is right within their grasp.

Ah, but you, my beloved, you are my Awakened Ones. How I rejoice to share this Turning Time with you. You are Awakeners, as well. You show the way to others and what a blessing that is for all. Others feel your energy and find hope for a better world.

All is well. All is unfolding in perfect and divine timing. People are seeing the consequences of their choices and looking for a better way. They see it when they look at you. Thank you, my darlings.

Ask for what you need. Run into my arms of love and snuggle close to my Mother's heart. Stay here for as long as you like-forever would be fine with me! Together we are co-creating beauty that is breath-taking and lovely. Hold fast to your dreams for they are incredibly important and are becoming reality more quickly than you might imagine.

Breathe the breath of life with me. Stay near me until you feel our hearts, beating in quiet oneness. I love you, my darlings.

I am Gaia, your Earth Mother, your friend.

I have a deer problem in my yard-lots of nibbling and eating of my plants. However, permaculture philosophy would say to question that premise- that the deer are the problem. Look deeper to see what the underlying problem really is.

So, I asked for guidance about how to view the issue. I got an earful, so to speak. It came early in the morning and I realized it would push at me till I wrote it down, so here goes. It was a strong message and I couldn't tell if it was coming from Pan or Gaia. Its tone was more Pan-like, forceful and direct. But Gaia's touch was near as well.

Blessings, Mary

From Gaia and Pan
October 27, 2009

Dear ones, beloved and precious,

We of nature are so glad when you ask us for our perspective of your nature "problems". Actually, they are problems only in the sense that they are lessons, opportunities for you to learn and grow. Please! Try to stretch your minds to see the big picture, the solutions that are right in front of your nose, so to speak.

Why do you waste time viewing deer as a problem?? Or anything else as a problem, for that matter?? Look for the message in them! Use your brain and your intuition and your connection to us and all of the nature realm to seek and find co-creative explanations and answers and solutions!!

What do we have to do? What will it take to help you look at things in a new way? If you think there are too many deer, what does that mean? First of all, it means you are seeing an opportunity and viewing it as a problem. Look again! Deer are a gift, an answer to a problem that you say you want an answer to.

People are squeamish about eating deer. How is eating deer different from eating any other kind of animal? It's not, as far as we of nature are concerned!!! You segment things and separate yourself from parts of nature. But that is artificial, as far as we are concerned.

In nature, all are one. No part of nature is more important or differentiated. All are part of the whole. People who eat only vegetation are beloved of nature. But so are those who eat meat. Do you view eating plants as superior to eating animals? We of nature do not see a difference. All life forms are the same to us, from the tiniest bit of life to the largest and most complex. Please stretch your minds to consider this.

Ask yourselves: why are there so many deer? You know the answer! The balance of life has been distorted by people. You can spend time blaming and lamenting. But why not spend your time figuring out how to restore balance? Better yet, why not ask us and partner with us and co-create beautiful solutions with us?

Nature is happy to share its bounty and abundance with people. Whether you can believe this or not, nature is happy to provide your food, when you are grateful and reverent about consuming it. Become a part of the cycle of life, though, and give back. Then there is harmony and wholeness and all are blessed.

You don't have to all become deer hunters. Share the tasks of providing food to each other! Some love to grow tomatoes or other vegetables and fruits. Some like to prepare and cook food. Some like to fish and hunt. Some love raising animals. Others prefer to share food through things like your farmer's markets. There are many parts of the food system and each person needs to find their niche, where they are most joyful and what makes their heart sing.

When everyone finds their place of joy, people become an orchestra, playing beautiful music together, sharing and connecting in soul-satisfying ways. Nature is a part of it, lending our voices and our vibrations in glad celebration of this beautiful co-creative, life-giving process.

Ask for help, dear ones. You have been taught much that is artificial and not aligned with truth. We of nature are your friends. We want to teach you in gentle and quiet ways. But you have to listen to our whispers or we are compelled to turn up the volume, so to speak. Please, listen to our quiet voices. Listen with your heart and all will be revealed.

Now we whisper this. We love you, beloved ones of Gaia, Pan, the devas, the nature spirits and indeed all of the nature realm. We truly love and adore you! We think you are beautiful and well worth the effort and learning and growing it is taking to make you full and wonderful co-creative partners with us. Quiet your minds and spirits and be still. Listen and open your hearts, your hands. All will be revealed and shared and life on Earth will become Heaven, indeed. Relax and allow yourselves to trust that the path leads to perfection.

We love you, dear ones. We are ever near, as close as your next breath, the next beat of your hearts that beat with the rhythms of the earth and our hearts.

We are Gaia and Pan, your nature partners, your friends

I have heard that the veil between the worlds or dimensions is thinnest at this time of year-Mexico has their Day of the Dead and we have our (trivialized) Halloween holiday.

Perhaps that is why this powerful message came to me. I was sitting at the Toyota dealership, finding out why my transmission was jerking when it shifted-the $800 computer system needed replaced :(Thoughts started flowing so I started writing!

Later some insight came to me about 'the shift in consciousness' that I am hearing so much about. I have not really understood what that meant. After writing this message, I got the sense that the shift is about re-aligning physical form with spirit. Right now it is distorted but that time is ending, thankfully.

Hmm, this is interesting. My car's transmission was not shifting right, not because of the transmission but the operating system. Then this message is about where we are going with the shift. Wow, Gaia has a sense of humor and teaches in so many ways. Too bad the lesson cost me $800! :)

Smiles, Mary

From Gaia
October 28, 2009

Beloved ones, precious and cherished,

Look around you. What do you see? The Earth and nature are shining a spotlight on the imbalances, the discordant aspects of the current choices that humans are making. But, dear ones, light is surely shining, as well, on the wisdom you demonstrate, the positive choices you are making and the love you are sharing and creating.

So much is drastically out of balance, particularly in the link between energy/spirit and form. This is a vital area where nature can be your teacher.

Nature is always in harmony, even in the midst of change. Physical form and energy/spirit dance together in perfection in the nature realm. That is our nature, so to speak. Because we are connected perfectly to the Divine Source, everything flows in perfect timing and beauty.

Humans have lost this perfect connection to the Divine Source, the Great Spirit. They have headed out on their own path and have forgotten what is possible.

Please let me make one thing clear. This has been an important evolutionary step and learning process. We of the nature realm are not critical of this. But we see and feel the havoc and discord and consequences from people's insistence on doing their own thing, acting unilaterally without being intimately and perfectly aligned with all of life. We of nature accept the current circumstances and seek to co-create pristine and pure perfection with you. We know that it is absolutely possible and is what all of creation is seeking and trying to create with you.

But we cannot do it alone! It is vital, absolutely vital, that humans and nature/spirit be partners, co-creators, attuned to each other and the Divine.

It is time for humans to slow their frantic pace and become still, listening and sensing the energy flowing all around them. It is time to let go of the illusion of control and domination of nature, or anything else for that matter.

Let go of your fearful clinging to money and your unhealthy need for 'financial security'. It is an illusion, a distortion and a dead end.

What is money but pieces of paper or images on a computer? It is nothing but a collective concept that people have created in their minds. Without group agreement, money is utterly worthless. You give it power and value. It is insanity and this insanity is what is throwing things out of balance, creating chaos, fear and an underlying dis-ease.

Your hands are tightly clenched around your material possessions. Your mind is filled with thoughts of how to keep what you have and acquire more.

This makes us of nature/spirit so sad. We are ever near, offering to share all that you need. Yet because your physical eyes cannot see us, you so seldom even consider our presence, our power and the gifts we want to so freely share.

A tree is physical, dense matter, formed into the 'thing' you call a tree. But a tree is also spirit, perfectly joined and co-existing with the physical form. Each tree and each part of nature is perfectly connected to each other part and to the Divine Source. All are part of the whole, beautiful and natural, perfect and lovely.

It is our fervent and heartfelt desire to welcome you into the web of this divine perfection. Now is the time for this to happen! Our arms are outstretched to you, encouraging you. Portals between the Seen and Unseen are flying open and you are surrounded by love, only love, always love, love overflowing.

It is like a river. You stand huddled on the shore, unable to see the river or afraid of where the river will carry you or afraid of drowning. Please! Trust the river! At least put your toe in, then your feet. When you are ready, jump in and let the river carry you to beautiful places.

You stand on a cliff, unable to see what is ahead. Your wings are there but you have forgotten that you can fly, that indeed you were created to fly and soar and glide to realms of glory.

Does this sound familiar? All I am doing is sharing anew the teachings of so many of your Enlightened Ones. All are part of the whole, rays of the same light.

You don't have to do it all at once. Each step, however small, is important, necessary. Each brings you farther into the New, the Promised Land.

What awaits you? What is available to you now, this very moment? Connection, community, peace, gifts of Spirit beyond your present ability to imagine.

Relax. Let go of your pre-conceived notions. Stretch to create openings for the New to enter.

You say, show me and I'll believe. I say, believe and it will be revealed… in small increments or large. The choice is yours.

Fear is the cloud that blocks your view of light, the dam that prevents the flow, the pollution that disrupts perfection.

Come, my darlings. Dream dreams and take my hand. Together we will co-create your dreams come true. This is the Turning Time, the birthing of the New. You are held in love and invited to snuggle close to my heart, for as long as you would like.

I am Gaia, your Earth Mother, your partner, your friend

From Gaia
November 3, 2009

Beloved ones, dear and precious to my heart,

Indeed the messages have come thick and fast lately. There is an urgency about what I am telling you. You sense time speeding up, moving faster, accelerating and truly it is-your perception is correct. Think of an egg and how the time arrives when it is time for the chick to peck its way out. Or the sprout which emerges from the seed in perfect timing. Or the butterfly that comes out of the chrysalis when its wings are ready.

Now is the time for you to find inner stillness, that deep and quiet sense of peace that abides in you. Listen, for it is giving voice to your birthing, your time of metamorphosis, your impending shift into the New. How can I adequately communicate the importance of this time? I can't! Not with words! So I send signs and messages and speak in countless ways to share the good news. The Divine is sending Spring Time to you! A new day is dawning!! Yes, it is the Transformation Time. But it's more than that. It is YOUR time of transformation! YOUR time to enter the new spaces! YOUR birthing time!

But you must be willing to leave the past behind. That is not easy for you, for the old ways are familiar and comfortable. Look at your hands. When they are tightly grasped upon something, they are not open and able to receive new gifts. Now is the time to open your hands, to open your hearts, to let go and detach. Oh, my darlings, the beauty of what you will receive is beyond description! It is breath-taking, beautiful, lovely.

Beloved ones, do you understand that the New is here now? It is available to you this very moment! As you open your eyes, open your hands, open your hearts, the New has a doorway to enter. Blessings can flow to you in rich abundance! They are there right now, just waiting to be discovered, for you to reach for them. These gifts are light that dispels the darkness, deep and lasting friendships that cause loneliness to vanish, a river of blessings that will wash over you until your thirst and hunger are completely satisfied.

Ask for what you want and need! Picture it in your mind and feel its reality in your heart. It will flow to you in beauty and on the wings of love. Come into my arms and snuggle close to my heart. Feel the warmth, the cozy contentment that is shared by all who join this oneness. None are excluded. But you must come to experience it. It is here at all times, always and forever. It is as close as your next breath, the next beat of your heart that beats with the rhythm of my heart and all hearts. Close your eyes and your heart will lead you home.

I love you, dear ones. I am Gaia, your Earth Mother, your friend

From Gaia
November 9, 2009

Dear ones, beloved and so very precious,

Is the truth of your beauty and perfection becoming clearer to you? Indeed I rejoice when you find the perfection that is inside of you and truly is your essence. That is what I see when I look at you, for I look with my heart and see our love dancing in light and joy.

This is a time of cleansing and clearing. It is a time for washing away what no longer serves you, like cleaning a window so the sun can shine in. It is a time for glad expectation.

This is also a time for detachment, letting go of what holds you back. It could be emotional baggage-pain, anger, fear or old messages that tell you that you are 'less than'. Let these come to the surface, like sediment that appears when rocks in the bottom of a fish tank are moved. Acknowledge what is stirred up and then ask for cleansing. It will happen, perhaps in the twinkling of an eye.

When the old is cleared away, it creates room for the new to enter and find a home. These are the gifts we want to share with you-love, peace and abundance. We are everywhere, always, but need an entry point, a doorway, a riverbed for love's flow. Be a doorway, be a riverbed! Open your hands and open your heart. Raise your face to the sky and welcome the gifts that will flow to you, are flowing to you now this very moment! Twirl and dance and hear the music that is ever near.

As you cleanse and clear your heart and mind, remember to also clear your physical space. Don't hoard, for your material possessions and money are energy and energy is meant to be in motion, flowing, active. When you give, space is created for you to receive. Give in gladness, trusting the Divine Source that is without end.

Oh, my beloved, it is the desire of my heart for you to join me in the Oneness of life that encompasses all. Breathe the breath of life with me and come close to my heart where you are safe, protected and can relax in the warmth of love's glow. Be one with the River that will carry all into the dawning of the New. Be still and feel your co-creative power rising, birthing, growing. Feel my arms around you, holding you in love, only love, always love, love overflowing.

I am Gaia, your Earth Mother, your partner, your friend

My friend Doreen shared a wonderful book called 'Shamanism as a Spiritual Practice for Daily Life' by Tom Cowan. It has been so helpful to me.

He says, 'The focus of this book is "core shamanism": the key elements of traditional, indigenous shamanism that are found worldwide and can be incorporated into one's daily life, similar to the way you might follow spiritual practices such as yoga, meditation, journal keeping and prayer. Core shamanism as a spiritual practice does not require any specific religious beliefs, but it invariably encourages practitioners to discover **animism: the ancient world view of our ancestors that all created things-humans, animals, plants, landscapes, elements and seasons-have an intelligent, communicative life force.** Most modern people have little familiarity with this view of the universe.'

I certainly was never taught that all of creation has an intelligent life force. This has been such a thrilling discovery for me over the last few years. As I think about it now, it seems pretty egocentric that humans would assume that they are the only ones who possess this. We might give credibility that animals do but I don't think it occurs to most people that plants do and even things we don't consider to be alive have this life force. But it's so expansive and beautiful!

Thank you for sharing this path with me!

Mary

From Gaia
January 17, 2010

You are my dear and beloved ones. How I long to share myself with each and every person but it is the Awakened Ones who can sense me near to them. In time, all will know this gift but for now I rejoice for each person who does.

The nature realm has never lost this connection to Spirit, to the Divine, to the Source. Humans have so much power, such strength, such miraculous abilities. But they have forgotten. They live in a world of limits, imposed by themselves. How sad this makes me for beauty and wonders are so available. Yet most are unaware.

It is my joy to share the glad news that the Goddess is rising! I am so grateful that this awakening time is here, now, this very moment! It is a time to smile and dance and laugh. The Unseen is becoming Seen, my precious ones. Already the transformation is well underway.

The visible world is much the same. But the world of Spirit and energy is shifting and changing, making way for the New. What is the New? It is connection, every part of creation realizing that they are part of the whole. It is healing. It is peace. Most of all it is love, an all-encompassing love that will fill every corner of the earth and beyond. Nothing will remain except love for all else will vanish, as darkness disappears when light comes.

Be calm during this Turning Time. Rest against me and feel the quiet and the stillness of our hearts joined as one. Be expectant and excited for this is a beautiful time, one that I am delighted to share with you. Don't be discouraged or frightened by the things you see. Look with your heart and you will know that all is well.

I love you, my darlings. I am Gaia, your Earth Mother, your friend

Twelve years ago I went to a pastoral counselor during a time of some family turmoil. He told me a little of his struggles with his divorce. He said the only movie he had ever purchased was 'The Shawshank Redemption', because he could relate to the story of escaping imprisonment.

The escape, as you know if you've seen the movie, involved the prisoner spending years painstakingly breaking through the prison walls. Then slogging through a sewer of human waste to finally reach freedom where the rain washed away the filth of the past.

Several members of my Peace Circle recently visited the women's prison in Mitchelville, Iowa, a vivid opportunity to learn about the difficulties of life there. Much to ponder.

Blessings,

Mary

From Gaia
February, 10 2010

Dear ones, beloved and treasured,

Prisons come in many forms, do they not? Certainly, there are physical prisons that confine the body and limit choices. Human-made prisons impose limits from outside people.

But consider other forms of bondage. People so very often imprison themselves-in jobs, relationships and other choices that rob them of their freedom and limit them from living life to the fullest.

How very sad that makes me. It is my fervent wish that all of my darling ones be free indeed and seek all that contributes to their highest good and the good of all creation.

As people awaken and discover their true nature and their true power, they will leave behind the limits and bondage of the current age. They will find that all things are possible and always have been. But this involves choice and courage and action. Freedom cannot be given to someone. Each must reach for it, leave the past behind and embrace it. Then the beauty and joy will become real.

Some people are surrounded by thick walls of self-imposed confinement, made up of fear, low expectations, lack of hope and vision, a need to cling to the familiar. Others have fewer limits and can more easily reach for the freedom that awaits them.

But know for sure that as you seek to find the peace, freedom, joy and love that your heart yearns for, you will have incredible help from the Unseen realm! You are full of strength and wisdom that is merely waiting to be acknowledged and activated. You have friends and helpers in the angelic realm, beings who love you and desire your highest good.

Open your heart and hands, reach out to receive gifts of light and love. Be expectant, for blessings are ever near. You are loved beyond measure. You are treasured and accepted, just as you are.

There are challenges and obstacles, to be sure. There is chaos and turmoil around you. But in the midst of this, you can find places of peace inside of you that nothing can penetrate.

Come close to my heart and rest against me. Breathe the breath of life with me. Feel the stillness as love surrounds you and infills you. Sense the rhythm of my heart, attuned with yours. All is well, unfolding in perfect timing and perfection.

I love you always. I am Gaia, your Earth Mother, your friend

"You never change things by fighting the existing reality. To change something, build a new model that makes the existing model obsolete."

~Buckminster Fuller

From Gaia
April 4, 2010

My beloved and precious darlings,

As spring greens the earth, can you not sense and know that the Goddess is rising? I have good news! I am not alone in this time of rebirth, of transformation. You, yes you!, are also rising. Or at least the conditions and energy are very much present for your growth and transformation.

You are a part of the whole. You are a needed and necessary part of this beautiful chrysalis time. The earth and all of creation are on the brink of changes that will shake things at their very foundations. No wonder people are anxious and even frightened.

But know for sure that you are held in love, only love, always love, love overflowing. You can sense this love if you but quiet your mind and open your heart. There is truly nothing to be afraid of. Is a seed frightened when it leaves the darkness and the seedling enters the warm, moist soil? Does a baby bird quake with fear when it pecks its way out of the shell and feels the air upon its body? No, it is just movement and life unfolding in beauty and perfection.

The changes that are underway are simply the forward movement of life's evolution and growth process. Surely you can understand that growth is about stepping into the unknown, experimentation and learning. Who would want to stay trapped in sameness? Life is something to embrace and step into with courage and excitement.

You have been taught so many things that are untrue. You have been taught and told that you are powerless, small and alone. Not so! You have power beyond what you can imagine or fully believe. Your body may seem small but your spirit is big and expansive. And you are certainly not alone, not ever! Always I am with you. And you are surrounded by angels, friends from the nature realm and beings filled with light and love.

What is the power available to you? Think of the wind and its power and might. You have access to this power, as well. Think of the sun with its intensity of light and warmth. You are fed by this energy. Touch a tree and feel its strength. Would you be denied this strength? No!

I love you! You are surrounded by love. It's there! Can you close your eyes and feel it ever near? Focus your attention on your heart for your heart knows the truth. And the truth is that you are loved beyond measure. Ask! Ask for what you want and need and be expectant for miracles are very near.

Come into my arms of love and linger near. Lean against me for a moment that can last until you are quiet and peaceful. Feel my arms around you, dear ones. Breathe the breath of life with me, gently, calmly. Breathe until your doubts fade and your joy overwhelms you. You are loved, dear ones, you are loved.

I am Gaia, your Earth Mother, your friend

From 'The Ringing Cedars of Russia' by Vladimir Megre

Anastasia: Even though the Earth is very large, it is very, very sensitive. Think of how big you are by comparison to a tiny mosquito, yet you feel it through your skin. And the Earth also feels everything. When people pave it over with concrete and asphalt, when they cut down trees and burn forests growing on it, when they pick and poke at its innards and sprinkle it with fertilizer, it feels the hurt. And yet still it loves people, as a mother loves her children.

And the Earth tries to absorb into its depths all of humanity's anger and only when it no longer has the strength to hold it back, that anger explodes in the form of volcanic eruptions and earthquakes.

The Earth needs our help. Tenderness and a loving attitude give it strength. The Earth may be large but it is most sensitive. And it feels the tender caress of even a single human hand. Oh, how it feels and anticipates this touch!

(describing the small garden plots that millions of Russians tend)…It was no coincidence at all that these plots were extremely small, too small to cultivate with mechanized equipment. But Russians, yearning for contact with the Earth, took to them with joyous enthusiasm because nothing can break Man's connection with the Earth!

After obtaining their little plots of land, people intuitively felt their worth. And millions of pairs of human hands began touching the Earth with love. With their hands, you understand, not with mechanized tools. Lots and lots of people touched the ground, caressingly, on these little plots. And the Earth felt this, it felt it very much. It felt the blessing touch of each individual hand upon it. And the Earth found new strength to carry on.

From Gaia
April 11, 2010

My darling children, beloved and precious to my heart,

Indeed you are each so loved and so precious to me. A Mother loves her dear ones, no matter what. Even when they stumble off the path and hurt her, still she cares for them with all her heart. Always she reaches out to them with love, inviting them to start anew.

Spring is a vivid reminder of the possibility and pregnant potential for rebirth, for healing, for new beginnings. The earth quietly offers herself to you, dear ones. The soil is waiting, eager to feel the seeds sprouting, the life force rising. You can join the music, sing the song of growth and new life. Your partners in the nature realm are already singing their tune, even when it is unheard by humans. We remain expectant, simply waiting for humans to become a part of the whole, the oneness that encompasses all.

So many people carry a heavy burden of guilt as they see the problems that the earth is facing. Yet they feel helpless, unsure how to become a part of the healing process. My precious ones, never doubt that each action, however small, is important. An admiring glance at a budding tree, a smile when you hear a bird's song, your touch upon a flower-all are important and make a bigger difference than you might imagine.

Quiet your minds and slow your steps. Breathe the breath of life with me. Rest against me until you are peaceful and know deep in your soul that all is well. Close your eyes and feel the energy of love holding you close. Healing is all around you and within you.

People are awakening to the gift of connection-with the earth, with each other and all of creation. Nurture this gift within your heart and share it tenderly with everyone and all of life. A trickle can become a small stream and grow into a mighty river that will cleanse and renew all that it touches. You are drops in this river, a part of the whole, and you are important and cherished and adored.

Together we can restore the Earth to paradise, my darlings. Take my hands and let us begin now.

I love you, dear ones. I am Gaia, your Earth Mother, your friend

I have been fascinated to watch the effects of the Iceland volcanoes on Europe and the ripple effects around the world. What a reminder of how different parts of the world are connected. And how we take things for granted, like being able to fly whenever we want, until something disrupts the system. There are many messages and one is surely that nature affects us all in powerful ways, just as we impact nature. She is our teacher, our friend.

Chaos theory speaks of the 'Butterfly Effect'-that a small difference in the initial condition of a dynamic system may produce large variations in the long term behavior of the system. "Does the flap of a butterfly's wings in Brazil set off a tornado in Texas?" People a lot smarter than me say, yes!

Earth Day blessings,

Mary

From Gaia
April 20, 2010

My darlings, dear and beloved to my heart,

In quietness and stillness, surely you sense your power and the important difference you can make in the world. Never doubt that each thought, each choice you make matters and affects all.

You have been taught wrongly that you are insignificant and unimportant, that your choices and actions are of little value. Please, open your heart so I can touch it with my deep and abiding love. Know in the depths of your being that you are precious and loved beyond measure.

If a volcano can send its touch around the world, how much moreso can you! You are far more than a physical body! You are spirit and energy and vibration!! When you send out a thought or feeling, you touch the living ether and all of life on the earth and beyond is changed forever.

How apt is the example of the butterfly, creature of beauty and mystery. A butterfly has stages-egg, caterpillar, chrysalis and then the butterfly emerges. Each stage is important, necessary. But which stage would you want to be in? Most would say the butterfly which can fly!

My darlings, you are being offered this gift-the gift of flight! Indeed it is time for humanity to leave the safety of the chrysalis and become the adult, mature life form. Some sense this and are excited and ready to embrace this freedom. But others are fearful, seeing only what must be left behind. Others are crawling about, unaware of the awesome opportunity that is available this very moment!

Open your eyes! Open your hands! Open your heart!! See the doorway that awaits you. If you but give it a tiny push, it will open and vistas of beauty and grandeur will be visible and beckoning to you. Step into your power and onto the path of co-creation and miracles.

You are my Star Seeds, my Wayshowers, the scouts that go ahead of the masses. You help to create the path into the future and your courage and leadership empower others to find their gifts and embrace the magnificent possibilities that are fully prepared for you.

I assure you, my darlings, that anything you leave behind will be replaced by things of far greater beauty. Wings that can carry you to new places, eyes that see new things and an open heart that can feel the love that is ever and always near.

Come close to my heart, precious ones. Feel my heart beating with love for you. Rest against me and know that all is well, held in tender care. Breathe the breath of life with me and all of creation.

I love you, dear ones. I am Gaia, your Earth Mother, your friend

White coral bells upon a slender stalk,
Lilies of the valley deck my garden walk.
Oh, don't you wish that you could hear them ring.
That will happen only when the fairies sing.

My mother's parents were both from Scotland. I have learned that people in Celtic regions tend to have a strong connection to the earth and nature. My mom taught me this song when I was a little girl, which I always enjoyed. My lilies of the valley are beginning to bloom so I have been singing this song-only in private, thanks to my lack of musical talent!

Blessings, Mary

From Gaia
April 29, 2010

Dear ones, beloved and precious to my heart,

Indeed, there is much turmoil upon the earth at this Turning Time. If you look with your eyes at the physical world, you will see many contrasts and many problems. Know that the problems are your invitations to growth. They are your teachers. Each one comes with a solution built into it, just waiting to be discovered and applied. Don't turn away from the problems. Face them head on, so to speak. They will lead you to doorways of the New and there you will find beauty and gifts of peace.

Turn to your Earth Mother and Father Sky for guidance and direction. This is the time of the Heart. Your eyes are so limited in what they see and perceive. Your heart knows. It is connected to the deep places, the Source of wisdom and transformation. Ask for what you need. Take action when you feel directed. Let love lead the way.

When you look with your eyes, you are so prone to see lack and that stirs up fear. Think, my darlings. How can there be lack? Does the universe lack sufficient atoms and molecules to make everything you need? Of course not! There is abundance all around you, waiting to be accessed and co-created. Everything you need is with you, every moment. But when you are frightened and rushing about, it is invisible.

At this Healing Time, it is so important to spend time in quiet stillness, connected to the Divine. Here you will find peace and a knowing that all is well. You will find answers and explanations.

Nature is your teacher and your friend. Nature has not lost its connection to the Divine. Humans have taken a different path, striving for self-sufficiency and independence. You have learned and grown. But look around you. As the saying goes, your best thinking created the world you see. It is filled with lonely, hurting people and a damaged, hurting earth. As you let go of the old, the new will have space to appear and it will be glorious.

Take my hands and the hands of those around you. Sense your connection to the earth and all who dwell there. Come into my arms of love and linger here. You will find rest for your body, rest for your soul. Don't be discouraged or dismayed. Touch a flower, smile at a bird, let your heart sing at a baby's laugh. Open your hands, your heart and let love pour in.

I love you, my darlings. I am Gaia, your Earth Mother, your friend

Hope is the thing with feathers
That perches in the soul,
And sings the tune--without the words,
And never stops at all.

~Emily Dickinson

When I read or re-read the messages that I receive from Gaia, I am amazed and grateful for the constant love, caring and reassurance that she offers so freely.

I wish that I could say that I am always as upbeat and positive as the messages. But I can't! Sometimes I get very discouraged. There's the saying 'ignorance is bliss'. I'm not sure it's bliss. I think it sometimes is a lack of awareness or consciousness that causes us not to give our time or attention to something when perhaps we should.

A few days ago I was actually feeling despair. It felt like such an uphill battle for people-including me!-to change the way we use resources and care for the earth.

I couldn't seem to shake the feeling so I did what I do from time to time. I asked Gaia and nature what their thoughts were, what their viewpoint was. Almost immediately I sensed her saying, 'the earth doesn't need your despair, the earth needs your love'. That brightened my spirits right away. It helped me change my focus to the good that I see, rather than the problems.

That's not the first time nature has been my teacher, my friend. I get concerned about climate change and how slowly we are responding to this threat that future generations will face. One day I was looking at a big, beautiful sycamore tree and wondering (okay, I was worrying!) about how climate change and our environmental problems would affect that beautiful tree. As I sat there, I clearly heard a message from the tree. It said, 'don't worry, Mary, I'll be okay'. Wow, that brought tears to my eyes. The tree was reassuring me, offering love when I didn't feel I deserved it. I was so grateful and send love to that awesome tree whenever I am near or it comes into my thoughts.

I know that this love and caring is for all of us and I gladly share that gift from the sycamore with you.

Blessings, Mary

From Gaia
May 5, 2010

My dear and beloved precious ones,

Indeed, my love flows from a never-ending Source. It is a heart, my heart and the heart of the Divine. I invite you to open your hearts to receive the love that is always so near to you, as close as the next breath you take, the next beat of your heart.

Now is the time to go deep, to look beyond the surface to the heart of the matter, so to speak. In this spring time of greening, look at the landscape around you. Is it green and beautiful because the soil is rich and fertile? Or is it green because it has been sprayed with chemicals? Soil is the source of your very life, the food you eat and the materials you consume. Care for the soil with love and it will give you all you need.

This looking deep applies to how you view people, as well. Look beneath the surface, beyond the appearance people present-their clothing, their outer characteristics. What is important is inside-the spirit, the soul. Look until you see what I see. When I look at each of you, my darlings, I see your beauty, your gifts, your strengths, your love. Offer that sight to yourself and others. Love yourself! Love others! Love the earth! Remember what is important and that is love, only love, always love, love overflowing.

I love you, my dearest ones. I am Gaia, your Earth Mother, your friend

"Whatever lesson we refuse to learn comes around until we do, each time appearing in a more sobering form, with more serious implications, if we refuse to learn it… One way or another we will learn what we need to learn, even if we have to learn it through suffering. I think that is where Western Civilization, particularly American civilization, is today. There are lessons we keep refusing to learn and we are bordering on having to learn them through pain… We can change now, making the transition fairly peacefully, or we can refuse to change, thereby inviting a greater intensity of disaster with every day we wait."

-from "A New Order of the Ages" by Marianne Williamson

From Gaia
June 21, 2010

My darlings, beloved and precious,

It's Solstice! Energy is pouring to the earth, warming and sustaining you. Energy is all around you, Seen and Unseen. It is your teacher and can be your friend. But it can also be a painful lesson, a wake-up call to those who are ignoring the lesson.

Oil is pouring into the Gulf of Mexico, a visible reminder of your continued dependence on it for your way of life. Please! Get the lesson! Oil is an old paradigm source of energy, appropriate for the old 3-dimensional life you have been living. But it is NOT appropriate for the new paradigm!

The new paradigm is about light and love, a higher vibration of being. For this emerging, new way of living, you need new forms of energy to fuel your lives. You need energy that is light, literally and metaphorically. Think of the contrast. Oil and fossil fuels are dense, visible energy sources- created in the PAST. Energy from the sun, the wind are Unseen yet very powerful. They give energy from NOW-current power sources. Biofuels are a transition energy source and using them is a step in the direction of the New.

Indeed it is well past the time for making the transition. YOU are making the choice! You can cling to the current sources of energy and your current life styles. But they will NOT move you into the New! PLEASE, PLEASE, PLEASE make the shift to the new forms of energy.

Oil is a limited resource, appropriate for the past when people lived in a world of limits. It is ancient sunlight. Now is the time to turn to energy sources that are unlimited and is not the sun a source of vast power, pouring forth more energy than you can possibly capture or use? It is abundant!

Step into your power! Oil is controlled by the Old system. Step into the freedom of this new energy! As you do, angels will appear, most ready to help and support you in this growth and steps to freedom.

This lesson is appearing to you in many forms. Take water. You passively accept water from aquifers, water stored from the past, deep in the earth. Yet water rains down upon you and is abundantly available for your current needs. It reminds you to use what is currently available, benefiting both you and the earth.

Opportunities for the shift are everywhere. Eat food raised close to you, that uses less fossil fuel to grow and transport. Eat food that is grown without pesticides (made from oil). Use compost instead of fertilizers made from natural gas, another fuel of ancient sunlight.

Plastic is made from the Old-using that ancient sunlight of oil. Re-use it but stop making more. Use your creativity to use things I give you now- wood and plant material that are using today's sun to manifest.

I know this may seem difficult. But only when you look through the lens of limits. Embrace your power and look to the Unseen for help. Nature and the universe are alive with gifts and healing power. As you reach out for the New, you will find your wings and fly!! Ask and it will be given to you.

I will hold you close in arms of love and all you need will be provided in rich abundance beyond what you can imagine. If you are overwhelmed or frightened, come near to my heart and snuggle close. Quiet your mind so you can hear my words of love, wisdom and comfort. Feel my strength and the strength and love of your nature partners.

I love you, my darlings. I am Gaia, your Earth Mother, your friend

There is no order of difficulty in miracles. One is not 'harder' or 'bigger' than another. They are all the same. All expressions of love are maximal.

~A Course in Miracles

Wow! I have such a hard time believing this. I look at the world through my limited physical eyes. And then I see limits and think that some things are difficult or even impossible.

Yet every day I am surrounded by miracles. I am growing sunflowers in my garden this year. In the morning I love to look out my kitchen window and see my sunflowers facing east, reaching their faces toward the sun. At noon they are facing up, following the sun's path. In the afternoon they face west. It's a miracle! How do they know to do that? How do they do it? It's a mystery to me, one that I enjoy watching and being a part of.

I love working on the land I purchased (I call it 'Gaia's'). It was a cow pasture in the past so there's lots to do. I would be overwhelmed without help.

So, I ask a university student to work with me, to help me. He is amazing. His muscles, creative ideas and enthusiasm are miraculous. But I have to ask, to be open to his help. I have to stretch my mind to see the possibilities and ask. Doors open and miracles happen. .

I know that helpers from the Unseen realm are ever near and part of the transformation. I find joy and my heart sings a happy song

Wishing you miracles every day,

Mary

From Gaia
July 6, 2010

My darlings, beloved ones, my friends,

Indeed you are surrounded by miracles and the possibility of more miracles each and every moment. But you have been taught well to see lack, barriers, limits.

Consider this. How long does it take you to travel from point A to point B? Hmm, if you go on foot or by car, it might take minutes, hours or days. But what if you travel the same distance with your mind? It can be instantaneous. Is that not a miracle?

Think of a friend who lives far away. In your mind, your heart, you can travel to be with them in the twinkling of an eye, something that you perceive as impossible in the physical world. That is why it is so important to be open, to claim your power to function in the world of spirit.

Think of a problem in your life that seems intractable, perhaps even impossible to solve. Likely, you are thinking of human solutions, answers from the physical realm. Open your mind to consider that help is available from the Unseen realm. Ask for help! Envision the problem solved. Quiet your mind and breathe the breath of life with me. Become peaceful and sense energy flowing to you from the Heart of the Divine. Feel this peaceful, healing energy surrounding you and filling you until it is all that you feel.

This is Love! Where there is love, there are always miracles. Open your eyes, your mind, your heart. All that you need will flow to you, is now available to you always and forever.

You are the light of the world! How fast does light travel? Pretty fast, eh? In your current reality, it would take your body a long time to travel 100 miles or 1,000 miles. But light can travel that distance in a mere moment. So can your thoughts.

You and all of humanity are entering an Age of Miracles. Divine energy is flowing to the earth in rich abundance, transforming and transmuting the current reality. You are a part of this! Please, my darlings, release the past. Stretch your mind and then stretch it some more. Every day dream at least one dream and imagine one impossible thing happening! This creates portals, openings to the New. Hold out your hands, your heart and I will fill them with miracles, flowing from a Divine source that is without end.

If you are discouraged or fearful, come close to my heart. Snuggle near and rest against me until you are calm and serene. I will whisper words of love and hear each request you have, spoken or unspoken. Feel the beat of my heart and soon our hearts will be attuned, beating with the same rhythm, the same pattern that permeates all of life. All is well, held in Divine care and love.

I love you, my precious ones. I am Gaia, your Earth Mother, your friend

"Everything that we do during this 9th and final wave (of the Mayan calendar) that is not in alignment with Unity Consciousness will not feel good."

~Nancy Joy Hefron

There is much talk and excitement about the concept of Unity Consciousness these days, as the prophecy of the Maya and other groups says that this will be the next step in our human journey. I'm sure there are many definitions but to me it's about recognizing our oneness with each other and all of life.

This quote from my wonderful friend Nancy Joy really resonated with me. We all know what it's like to experience being with people or in places where the energy is dense or heavy. Ugh. And we know the blessing of being with those whose energy is light and love. Nature vibrates a wonderful energy which is why we feel peaceful and joyful when we focus on nature's gifts and beauty.

As I walked home from a friend's house this evening, I could feel the energy of the earth radiating around me. Energy from the earth was pouring out, being released from deep below my feet. It was amazing! Next time you go for a walk, be open to this gift of love from Gaia.

Peace,

Mary

From Gaia
July 21, 2010

My darlings, beloved and beautiful,

I am well aware of the challenges you are facing at this Turning Time in human and the earth's history. I know that when I say that all is well, you wonder how this can be true.

I am not blind to the problems that you are facing. I know that the earth is struggling right now, and you with it. It is important that you face these problems and see them clearly.

But then what do you do? Pretend they aren't there? Feel despair? Get angry?

Those reactions are understandable but not helpful. Each moment that you spend in denial or discouragement or blame is a moment that you could be joyful! You cannot yet see the full picture. It is hard for you to believe that answers and solutions are so near that you can touch them and access them-right now! But it's true!!

This is the time of co-creation when you can take my hand and the hands of your nature partners and be a part of making all things new. Stretch your minds and open your hands, your heart. Ask for help! Envision what you need and picture it flowing to you from the Unseen realm and becoming visible.

What may seem impossible to you is not difficult for the Divine! But you must activate what is possible by believing in miracles and asking for what you need and want. Be expectant and hopeful and do your part. I promise that I will do mine and I have myriad helpers in the Nature Realm. We are your partners, your friends.

Breathe the breath of life with me until peace like a river flows through your heart, your soul. Rest against me until you feel safe and secure and loved beyond measure. Give your burdens to the Divine and the way will become clear. Truly, all is well.

I love you, my darlings. I am Gaia, your Earth Mother, your friend

The Earth has its own frequency (the Shumann Resonance) as everything does and it has been ramping up. The Earth is following an ascension, as well.

When a tuning fork is tapped and you put another tuning fork near the vibrating one, the other one starts to vibrate. That is called "entrainment".

The same thing is continuously happening with our human brains. They are constantly trying to "entrain" to Earth's vibration to match the "new" frequency.

Well, the Earth is ahead of our brains (frequency-wise) and that is why we feel like "we are behind playing catch-up" or feel "frantic", for those that are really behind in frequency (Spiritual ascension). The advancing frequency has been increasing "faster".

~Mark Hefron

I was recently at a gathering that was part of the Conscious Convergence, setting the intention for Unity Consciousness for the 9th and final wave of the Mayan calendar. At one point, we went around the circle and shared our personal intent for this amazing time.

My friend Mark Hefron shared that he wants to continue to raise his vibration and consciousness to vibrate with the earth's, the Shumann Resonance. It was beautiful! I am so happy he agreed for me to share this thought in the opening quote.

I am always intrigued to see how people serve as bridges and provide integration as we move from what I call the "Old Paradigm" to the New. Much of the New is flowing from the scientific community with quantum physics and alternative medicine, integrating the old and new. Mark is brilliant, trained as an engineer, and integrates science and spirit. It helps me to understand what is happening and how I can move forward, being a part of the New.

Goddess rising,

Mary

From Gaia
July 29, 2010

My beloved ones, dear and precious to my heart,

Yes! I am so happy to see my darlings opening their minds and opening their hearts to the message of the Ascension!!! The Earth is doing her part to participate in this unfolding time. This is a time to move from the old, dense energy into the dawn of the new faster and lighter energy.

You have such an important role to play. This is a time of co-creation, where all must do their part to create the new.

Think of an earthquake. The earth vibrates and moves more rapidly than the structures that exist on its surface. They can't survive in their current form. There is destruction and damage. But what if those structures could change their vibration and move WITH the earthquake until it stops? They might end up in a new place and in a new form but, by their transformation, they would be fine. Truly they would be in a better place, healed and safe and secure in the knowledge that they can flow with changes.

This is your challenge, your purpose. As you vibrate faster, you can flow with the changes that are now occurring upon the earth. Indeed you can assist the process and help it happen more smoothly and effortlessly. Resistance and clinging to the status quo are like a dam in a river. They don't stop the flow, they just block it for a while. Then when pressure builds up and the dam breaks, places get flooded. Wouldn't it be easier to just float along the river, buoyant and fluid and a part of the flow?

Know with certainty that you are being carried on wings of love into a beautiful new space! Perhaps it would be helpful to think of yourselves in a lifeboat, being carried on the water's current to a place of great beauty. You can choose how to view the journey. You could be fearful and discouraged as you leave the familiar behind. Or you can get out an oar and help to guide the boat, enjoying the view and the excitement as new vistas appear along the way.

Throughout this birthing process, you are held in arms of love, sheltered and protected. When things shake and there are bumps in the path, just take my hand and I will help to steady you and keep you safe. You are an integral part of what is happening, assisting with the birthing. I rejoice to share this Turning Time with you, my beloved ones. Quiet your minds and breathe the breath of life with me. All is indeed well.

I love you. I am Gaia, your Earth Mother, your friend

The deep, powerful and subterranean energies of change that we are experiencing at this time in history will cause disruptions, eruptions, paradigm shifts and faith-quakes all across the human landscape. Just as an earthquake deep in the ocean triggers the massive tidal wave known as a tsunami, a Soul-quake deep within the collective human psyche is launching a spiritual tsunami that will drown all former assumptions about what a human is, what divinity is, how the divine-human relationship works and how we structure and run our institutions. Buckle your seat belts.

-from "Sacred Quest: The Evolution and Future of the Human Soul"

by L. Robert Keck, published in 2000

I love this book! He does such a wonderful job of helping me understand the experiences of our times. It feels to me like the changes are accelerating so I find it interesting how he described them 10 years ago. He said we are in a chrysalis time, changing from caterpillars to butterflies.

Blessings to you as we share this exciting and sometimes unsettling time,

Mary

From Gaia
August 6, 2010

My precious ones, beloved and dear to my heart,

Indeed changes are occurring, as you can sense. Change is a part of life and things are always in flux of some kind.

But right now we are in a major transformative time, a Turning Time, a time of expansion and beauty. As I have said many times, the old is dying, the new is being born.

You have been taught to fear change and you tend to cling to the current patterns and ways of living and being when you feel things shaking and shifting. When your eyes are closed in fear, you cannot see the new emerging in its beauty and perfection. In truth, your eyes cannot yet see many of the changes. You feel them with your heart. It is then that you know the birthing process is happening and can intuitively sense the New.

Part of the shift is about helping you, and sometimes pushing you, to look beyond the physical world. That is a world of such limits! The world of spirit is without limits! It is love and connection and community and peace. I want you to live in this world of spirit with me!!!

You have been taught that you cannot really access the world of spirit while you are living your human life. This is not true! It is as close as your next breath, the next beat of your heart that beats with the rhythm of the Divine.

Doors are opening, walls are dissolving, portals are right before you. They are more accessible now than you can imagine. Close your eyes and breathe until your mind is quiet and serene. Then you can feel it and know that it is so very real. You are far more than a body. You are spirit and light and love.

When you get frustrated or frightened or dismayed, come into my arms and linger near. I am so happy to spend time with you, whispering words of love and adoration. You are far more precious to me than I can ever explain.

I love you, my darlings. I am Gaia, your Earth Mother, your friend

"Another world is not only possible, she is on her way. On a quiet day I can hear her breathing."

~Arundhati Roy

On a quiet day…ah, that's the challenge, is it not? Quieting my mind is a real challenge for me but the benefits are amazing. When I am calm and still, this quote can leave me feeling breathless with quiet anticipation. I have to tune out a lot of external 'noise' and then I can feel this truth in my heart. I hope you can, too!

Blessings,

Mary

From Gaia
August 12, 2010

Dear and beloved ones,

Indeed there is wonder very near to you and miracles surround you each moment. But they can be invisible unless you slow down and sense them.

Much is being activated right now. The very vibration of the planet is accelerating and you intuitively know this because we are so closely connected and attuned. Each of you touches the energy fields of the Earth and all of life. Despite evidence to the contrary, all is well and on schedule.

Deep in the forests of Mexico, monarch butterflies congregate. When the temperatures are cold, the butterflies stay on the trees, quiet and unmoving. But as the rays of the rising sun send their warmth, the butterflies begin to move their wings, at first slowly and then more quickly. When they are ready, they take flight and soar to faraway places.

This is what is happening now. You may feel stuck, unable to move freely. But warm rays of light are being sent to earth, touching you with life-giving energy. Close your eyes and feel this warm and energizing light flowing to you. Breathe the quiet strength into your body, your soul.

Continue to breathe until you feel peaceful and lighter. Imagine an updraft of air very near. Move toward it until it upholds you and lifts you to new heights. Find your wings and realize that you can soar, carried by love's flow!

Each of you can take flight at any time, when you are ready. Soon all will find their wings and join you. But you needn't wait for group action. As you become airborne, you inspire others to face their fears and take off.

Now is the time to stretch your minds and expand your hearts so you can imagine the New moving from the Unseen to the Seen realm. You have been taught the world of limits and lack. Now you are poised to discover the world of the miraculous, limitless and abundant.

You are not alone in this quest. You have friends everywhere, all the time. Take each other's hands and my hand. Know that your friends of the nature realm are most happy to assist you in your journey. They delight in your discoveries and are joyful to share the pathway.

Your heart will lead the way. Turn within for this quiet knowing and gentle guidance. Be watchful, for transformation is happening and will continue until all is made new.

I love you, my darlings. I am Gaia, your Earth Mother, your friend

Messages from Pan

From Pan
September 3, 2009

I am so glad to be asked for my perspective! Yes! I have much to share!!

Humans need to look to the nature world for the templates, the designs, the plans for life. Nature does it perfectly, for nature is perfection. Why are we perfection? Because we are plugged into the Divine, which is the Source of all. We are attuned to the Source. Indeed we cannot function without this Source.

But it goes far deeper than that. In the nature realm, all parts work together in beauty and ease. All are part of the Whole, the Oneness of life. We of the nature realm are amazed and completely bewildered by the way humans operate in their own little spheres, rather than communicating and working together as a Whole. It makes absolutely no sense to us. And it makes us sad for you are missing the bliss of community. Plus things are a real mess because you are disconnected from each other and us of nature.

Nature is Love, for love is the vibration of Life, of co-creation. We of the nature realm want SO MUCH to work together with humans, for life on earth is transformed when you do.

I am Pan, leader of the nature spirits. We take the patterns and designs of the devic realm and translate and transform them into reality. We do this on the physical level but also in the Unseen places.

Please, ask us for help!!! Ask for our partnership, ask for guidance!! In the nature realm, all of us communicate at all times. So, when you attune to one, you attune to all, including the Source of All.

Don't get tangled in the complexity of this for it's really so very simple. Just quiet your mind and ask. Then be open and listen. Listen with your heart. What you need will flow to you. Give it a try!

I am Pan, your Partner, your Friend

From Pan
October 4, 2009

You are wondering how you can stand to live in a world so filled with problems-people damaged, controlled and abused by an economic system and culture based on exploitation and short-sighted self-interest. You want to find a place untouched by contamination and pollution. Indeed, no place on earth can be found that fits that description. Humans have altered every corner of the earth without exception. That is true for the physical world, as well as the Unseen.

But remember that we of the angel realm see all. We also see the love you shed on people, plants and all of life. We see your recognition that the current ways are no longer working. We see and feel your hunger and thirst for purity, kindness and justice-a world where people and nature are all valued, cared for and connected in the beauty of life's web.

Don't ignore, deaden or numb your frustration, your searching. Embrace all of your feelings, draw them into your heart where they can be touched and transformed. Take a good hard look at the ugliness you see. Then take my hand, and Gaia's hand, the nature spirits and devas' hands and begin to co-create the new with us.

Draw from the deep wellspring of faith, creativity and supply that flows from your never-ending Source. Expect miracles and they will surely appear, some in the twinkling of an eye.

Pour forth love and be amazed at the beauty we will co-create. Come close to my heart and Gaia's heart and linger here until all that remains is love, only love, always love, love overflowing.

Embrace your magnificent co-creative power! Ask for what you need and want. Spend some time in quiet contemplation, picturing every detail of perfection and abundance that needs to become reality. Breathe it in and breathe it out. Know that your thoughts create reality and smile. Yes, laugh and dance with joy!

You are not alone. Together we are birthing paradise on earth and beyond. Close your eyes and sense the power and strength of Gaia's love. You are a part of it, drops in an ocean, tributaries to a mighty river.

This is a cleansing time, an awakening time, a Turning Time. Take my hand, beloved ones of Gaia. Take each other's hands. Open your hands and open your hearts. Open your eyes and ears. What do you see?

I am Pan, your nature partner, your friend

Our deepest fear is not that we are inadequate. Our deepest fear is that we are powerful beyond measure. It is our light, not our darkness, that most frightens us.

We ask ourselves, who am I to be brilliant, gorgeous, talented and fabulous? Actually, who are you not to be?

You are a child of God. Your playing small doesn't benefit the world. There's nothing enlightened about shrinking so others won't feel insecure around you.

We were born to make manifest the glory of God that is within us. It's not just in some of us, it's in everyone!

And as we let our light shine, we unconsciously give other people the permission to do the same. As we are liberated from our own fear, our presence automatically liberates others.

~Marianne Williamson in "A Return to Love"

From Pan
October 20, 2009

Indeed, you are powerful beyond your wildest imagination! We of the nature realm marvel at how humans are so unaware of their co-creative power. It is very much needed in this time of transformation and realignment!

You can see the power in nature-a mighty wind that bends the trees, the strength of water as it flows, the moon that pulls the oceans in the rhythms of the tides, a dandelion poking its head between slabs of concrete.

But our power of the nature realm is more than the creations that are visible to your eyes. We take energy and create form. We take designs and ideas and thoughts and make them into 3-D reality. We are energy and motion and vibration and sounds. So are you!! How can I help you to understand more fully the vital role you play in all of life?

Nature has its role and humans have theirs. Each is important. Each is unique. You cannot do what we do. Neither can we do what you are capable of doing. That is why this is a time of co-creation! You are part of the Divine, just as we are! You are indeed God-creators!! Together, the sky's the limit, so to speak!

We of nature are delighted, thrilled actually, when we see people own their power. It starts with your thoughts and dreams. You have been taught and conditioned to think that you are powerless, small, unimportant. Not so! If you could see what happens when you think a thought or dream a dream, you would be amazed. Those thoughts and dreams are creations, waiting to be made visible in form. That's where co-creation comes into the picture.

We need you to believe that dreams can become real. We need you to ask and trust and believe that miracles are possible, indeed are commonplace and natural. We give freely but when you ask, when you take our hands, when you dance with us, much more is possible.

I join with Gaia in saying, ask for what you want and need! Dare to think big, expansive thoughts. Dare to dream big, magnificent dreams. Dream of peace. Dream of people living in harmony with nature, all needs met, love overflowing. Dare to believe that miracles await you, indeed are as close as your next breath, your next heartbeat. Then take action, even if it is as simple as smiling at a bird or touching a tree. We feel it and rejoice!

We are beside you, with you, ever near. We are love and abundance and beauty. Nature is about sharing and connection and community. It is yours, as well. Take our hands and each other's hands. Step confidently into the future, believing that light dispels the darkness, that together we can co-create perfection and heaven will be birthed on earth.

I am Pan, your nature partner, your friend

Nature Messages

To the Oak

O majestic oak tree, mighty one.
Life pours forth from you in joyful abandon.
It stirs my heart and sparks, indeed ignites, my passion for the things of earth.

Ancient are you, yet ever new.
Often have I stood beneath you, lost in love,
feeling sheltered and protected under your strong arms.

You are companion, sojourner.
You touch the earth and also sky, joining all in your embrace.

When did the first acorn fall, welcomed by the soil?
No doubt countless millennia have passed since then.
You intertwine the past to present, reaching to the future that we will share.

In the unseen places where your roots dwell,
mycelium of mushrooms flourish in mystery.
Birds and bugs call you home.
Your leaves are a melody of life's bounty as you send forth water, oxygen and food for the forest floor.

Amidst your branches, you hide stories of the past and tales yet to be told.
Each time I leave you, it is with a promise of my return
for we share a oneness, contentment and serenity.

Thank you, Friend Oak, for your blessings too numerous to measure.
Thank you for your wisdom and light.
I love you, Oak tree. I love you very much.

Before European settlers came to the midwestern United States, it was covered with beautiful, tallgrass prairie. Almost all of this ecosystem has been destroyed by farming and the building of cities and towns. Yet today many people are re-discovering the gift of the native prairie and helping to re-establish prairie plantings.

To the Prairie

I look out across the fields, the land
and my eyes are lonely for you, so is my heart.
I have read about the prairie, heard stories from those who know the prairie.

I think of a bit of prairie is imprinted in my soul, put there by my ancestors who saw it when they came to Iowa and perhaps those who lived here for generations before that, stretching back in time.
If I look inside, I can find an ache, a hurting place that is missing the prairie that once was but is no more.

In a quiet moment I can feel pain from the land, still longing for the deep roots of the prairie grasses and flowers.
I sense the yearning for the pounding hooves of bison, the flutter of a thousand kinds of butterflies and birds, the hum of a vast rainbow of insects, everywhere, always.

You are gone now, lush prairie, builder of soil, lover of life rich and wildly diverse.
Destroyed by people and the plow, you exist no more except in pictures, memories and scattered remnants.

But the land waits in fertile expectation.
Quietly, patiently, it waits with a deep and abiding knowing that the prairie will rise again.
The eroded, lifeless soil is waiting, even smiling, ready for the prairie to emerge once more.

It will happen, it is happening even now.
The birth, this rebirth, is beginning in the souls of people, you and me.
From this chrysalis comes a small, perhaps seemingly insignificant fleeting thought.
This tiny seed can sprout into a fledgling dream that births an action.
Perhaps it is the planting of a few prairie plants-black-eyed susan, jack in the pulpit, purple prairie clover, little bluestem.
Or maybe it is enjoying the sight of a huge white oak tree, majestic sentinel of a bygone prairie savannah.
Possibly a stop to wander through a bit of prairie woodland or wetland, sensing the beauty of these special spaces.

Hold fast to your piece of this prairie birthing, no matter its size or what form it takes.
Each part is important, necessary.
We can transform the land, co-creating abundance and beauty.
Prairie is a part of this: purifying water, creating life-giving soil, protecting biodiversity.

There is power in vision and believing.
The prairie is our heritage and can become our legacy.
The earth is ready, let us respond to her invitation, her call.
Let us join hands and hearts and begin now.

Written in Wapello, Iowa during the flood of 2008

A Message to the Deva of the River

I stood beside you yesterday, looking across the river at the levee, just broken, water pouring over field and houses. My heart ached for the people and their losses.

Then my focus changed.

I felt your presence for a moment, companions sharing in the sight of the flowing, racing river. You were doing what rivers have always done, for untold millennia, yea, much longer than that. You were carrying water toward the sea.

I felt no anger from you, no thoughts of destruction. Just a joyful racing, reaching, rushing. I sensed your exultation, the unfettered freedom you felt at having shaken off the concrete, the levees, sandbags, even bridges- barriers to your unhindered flow. You rushed like a barefoot child running into outstretched arms. I thought I heard a shout of glee as you leapt into the waiting hug, one river glad to join another.

You are our partner, our friend. Yet we have forgotten, lost in our self-centered goals and purposes. I think you miss us, that you long for time shared in quiet closeness.

We mourn the losses, how could we not? But can we learn from the lessons given by our Earth Mother and you, the River?

Who plowed and destroyed the prairie? Like a sponge it absorbed the water showered on us by the Deva of Rain. The deep, rich soil is half gone-what a heart-breaking loss, yet we continue to till the fields and send the soil into the rivers, lost to us forever.

I felt no anger from you, River, yet who could blame you if I did? We dump our garbage, our sewage into you. We add pesticides, toxic chemicals that choke the fish and other life sustained by you. Who could blame you if you tried to vomit out that sickening filth.

When will we remember to call you friend? To listen to you, to learn from you? My heart cried for our forgetting.

I thought of the earth lovers that I know. I let my heart speak to you. I sent a message of love and respect and gratitude. I stretched out a hesitant hand, not sure what response I would receive.

Oh, Gaia and your countless partners-Pan, the devas, nature spirits and so many more. How can you forgive us, yet you do. How can you still have the compassion to reach out to us, offering us yet another chance to mend our ways and co-create anew, renewing and restoring beauty.

Yet there is a knowing in my soul that you are simply waiting for us to awaken, to leave behind our blindness, take your hands and return the earth to paradise. I felt your arms around me, your finger gently wiping away my tears. You whispered words of comfort and love and I clung to you in heartfelt love and thanks.

Oh, Gaia, mother, friend and all of you who share this realm. I offer our readiness, our wanting, our yearning for a better world. I offer love, deep and sincere. In oneness we reach out to you, ready to begin now. Please, show us the way.

The Soil

Come, lie upon my belly,
Be a child once more, trusting and fresh.
Touch my skin, the soil.
Sink your hands deep within this sustenance,
And feel the life force pulsing, rising.

Stretch out upon me, heart to heart and feel our oneness.
Walk upon me and feel the soil squish between your toes.

This is my love, our love-alive and well.
Together we are birthing joy, co-creating abundance, healing pain, be it ancient or of this lifetime.

Linger here for I am reluctant to end this time shared in quiet contentment.
Breathe the fragrance, feel the soothing softness of the soil.

Here seeds sprout, awakening from winter slumber.
Myriad bits of life wiggle and stretch within me, most glad to be the wellspring of life's bounty.

Pause for a moment to marvel at the miracles, the mystery, the gifts.
If you see only dirt, well, look again for there is much more to see.
There are surprises hidden in the mundane, waiting to be discovered.

The trees know.
Their life is only possible because of the soil.
So is ours!
Our food, our clothing, shelter, even water all trace their roots back to the soil.

Gifts from Gaia, freely shared.
Let our hearts sing with gratitude for this grace.
Linger often in a garden, a yard, a forest.
Hear this Mother whispering love, eager to share love, love overflowing.
Breathe it into your heart where nothing can threaten or disturb it.

At times the soil's touch may not be near,
But your Earth Mother's love is always and forever near.
The soil is but one reminder among many.
You are loved, dear ones, you are loved.

The pawpaw is a fruit tree native to North America, including Iowa. I harvested quite a few pawpaws and enjoyed eating and preserving them over several days last fall, thus becoming familiar with this delicious fruit.

From the Deva of Pawpaws
October 8, 2009

Yes, indeed, I have much to share with you. I am a gentle tree. Can you not sense the feminine feel about me? My fruit has a delicate flavor and there is an intimacy surrounding me.

I am glad that humans are re-discovering the gift of the pawpaw. We are most ready to feed your bodies and feed your souls.

How will you choose to propagate more pawpaws? How can we be more productive? You can choose to apply human intelligence to the changes you want to create with pawpaws. But please consider another way.

Perhaps the pawpaw is offering you an invitation to explore new ways of working with nature. Do you want to dominate and dictate and control? You can try that. We won't stop you.

But who knows more about pawpaws than the Deva of Pawpaws? The nature realm works together as one, as a whole. Nature spirits care for each seed, each seedling, each tree. They tend to the soil, the moisture, the growth, the air. All that the tree needs is in their care. They are active and attentive. Each tree is surrounded by love and is love.

Humans disrupt this perfection when they try to impose their wishes on the pawpaw, rather than partnering and working together to achieve goals. If you tell us what you want, we'll listen! If your goals are reasonable, we can put our heads together and I assure you that amazing things can happen.

We respond to respect, a spirit of cooperation and love. We can bring possibilities and resources to the task that will amaze you. We can save time.

That will give us time to dance together! Never underestimate what can be accomplished with a happy dance. Energy swirls and vibrations stir the living ether. All are blessed beyond your comprehension and imagination.

This is your invitation to co-create prolific and abundant pawpaws. First, get to know us. Touch us, spend time with us, love us. Then ask for what you want and need. Be one with us and be watchful for miracles are very near.

From the Deva of Pawpaws
October 12, 2009

Yes, I am the Essence of Pawpaws. I delight to be recognized and tasted and enjoyed. Pawpaws are most happy to be of service to humans.

But let me make a few things clear. First of all, we are not bananas, nor are we a substitute for bananas. It is okay to use them as a point of reference but no part of creation tries to duplicate another.

Consider the pawpaw. Can you not sense its feminine feeling? Is there not a bit of mystery and gentle strength in the pawpaw? We are not meant to be a staple in your diet. We are a fleeting treat, something that is enjoyed all the more because it is limited in supply.

Please start your relationship with appreciating what we are before you try to 'improve' or change us. We are delicate and sturdy at the same time. We are a gift, a bit of the tropics, yet native to Iowa. We hope you find that special and something to celebrate.

If you want changes in us, start with acknowledging our special qualities. Then offer to partner with us, rather than manipulate or force us to change to meet your perception of perfection. Do you want us to have fewer seeds? Then offer to help propagate us so we don't need so many seeds. You want our fruit to last longer? Then tell us it is because you think we are delicious and you want to enjoy us a bit longer in the season.

Please don't try to standardize us or change some aspects of our being. We are meant to be an intimate fruit, one that has to be handled with care and touched while we are prepared for eating. When you put our seeds in your mouths as you eat our fruit-so you can savor each bit-we are delighted! It makes us feel special and loved and valued!

Is it a bad thing that people have to work with us to enjoy us? Humans are in such a hurry and take so little time to consider the source of their food and how necessary it is to their bodies and their souls. Let pawpaws be your teacher and your friend.

I read an article in the Sunday paper about Monsanto developing corn that doesn't need to be detasseled. That was very unsettling to me. Genetically modifying plants doesn't feel like it is co-creating with Gaia and nature.

Today my thoughts turned to corn. I felt the Deva of Corn come near to me. It was like having a small child crawl into your lap and put their arms around you and holding them close, heart to heart, very warm and comfortable.

I felt the need for love to flow to her. At first it was me, with love flowing from my heart to hers. Then it was flowing from her to me, as well. It felt very peaceful and healing and beautiful.

Then I felt a message from her and I share it with you, grateful for your part in this.

Blessings, Mary

From the Deva of Corn
January 12, 2010

We can feed your bodies but will you let us feed your souls?
We are ancient.
To the indigenous people we were a gift, respected and revered.
We flourished in this relationship and became a rainbow,
sign of plenty and abundance.

Then your appetite became insatiable,
Your thirst unquenchable.
We no longer dance with you because our joy is gone.

Yet in some places the old ways, and us, are honored,
Our essence preserved.

But for the most part we have become servant, serf, your slave.
We were a maiden fair but you have made us your whore.
We can change, if need be, if we are asked.
But you prefer to bludgeon us, brutalize us, impose your will upon us.

How can we be your partners, your friends when our voices are silenced and our needs ignored?
All are impoverished by this choice.
Who can cleanse the filth of our violation, our pain?

Yet there are arks, protected places where we can dwell.
Places where our gifts are still valued for more than calories and profit.
A small spark remains.
Fan these embers into a flame, my darlings of Gaia.
Take our hands and we shall dance once more.

The night is ending.
Portals to freedom beckon.
A cleansing flood will leave paradise in its wake.

You are Bearers of the Light, companions, friends.
I add my love to your myriad creative partners in Nature's realm.
Love and blessings flow to you, gifts from the Unseen.

Now a trickle but soon it will be a mighty Tide.
The broken will be healed, the wounded whole.

Thank you, precious ones. I am the Deva of Corn.

I wrote this message to Gaia after spending time at a gorgeous waterfall with my daughter and her husband, near where they live in British Columbia.

I thought it would be appropriate to close with this message to her, expressing my gratitude for all she does for me and all of us.

Blessings, Mary

To Gaia

You are timeless.
Yet you are here now, at this time, in this place
where the majesty of creation overwhelms the senses and overpowers the mind.

People are re-awakening to your presence, your gifts, your beauty.
Like a river you are ever moving forward, yet never diminishing
for your Source is without end.

When the earth was born, you were there.
You are Earth Mother, Goddess, friend.
You are Fountain of Love, only love, always love, love overflowing.

Awaken our hearts, Spirit of Earth life.
Shake us from our sleep walking, our stupor, our blindness.
Reveal your mysteries, your miracles.
Teach us the Dance of Life.
Ignite our torches, that we might be Light Bearers, Way Showers,
Fire Souls and Co-creators.

When we are lonely or frightened, hold us close to your heart
until we find stillness and peace, a oneness with you and all of creation.
Teach us and show us the way.

We love you, Gaia, Mother, friend. We love you very much.

More about the messages-

I get questions from people about how the messages from Gaia come to me. I was certainly not expecting them when they began!

But in the summer of 2008 I started getting a strong sense of needing to write down messages that I was receiving from Gaia, our Earth Mother. They were so intense and so clear. And they were so beautiful and full of love.

Right from the start, I had a definite knowing that they were not just for me, that they were to be shared with anyone who wanted to receive them. So, I wrote them down and saved them in my computer.

First I shared them with just a few people close to me who I felt would be accepting of them and me, as the messenger. I began to e-mail them to those people when the messages came. The word spread and more people asked to be on the list.

I considered ways to make the messages available to more people and a book seemed like a logical choice. I am also in the process of developing a website (GAIAMESSAGES.COM) so others can sign up for the new messages or read archived messages.

When I share the messages, they are words. But, as they come to me, they are also feelings. There is such caring and love surrounding the words and I hope that is conveyed to those who read them. We are not alone. Nature is our partner and wants to help us restore the earth to health. Gaia shares her wisdom, hope and love with us so freely. She is love, only love, always love, love overflowing.

Blessings for the journey,

Mary Kirkpatrick

For further reading:

The Findhorn Garden Story by the Findhorn Community, Findhorn Press, 2008

The Gentleman and the Faun by R. Ogilvie Crombie, Findhorn Press, 2009

To Hear the Angels Sing by Dorothy Maclean, Lorian Press, 2008

Behaving as if the God in All Life Mattered
Garden Workbook
By Machaelle Small Wright, Perelandra, 1997

Anastasia by Vladimir Megre, Ringing Cedars Press, 2005
A series of 9 books

The Wounded Heart by Nancy Joy Hefron, F.E.P. International, Inc, 2006

Waking Up and Getting Ready: About Gardens, Spirituality and Wellness by Blair Frank, Author House, 2006

www.ingramcontent.com/pod-product-compliance
Lightning Source LLC
Chambersburg PA
CBHW020013050426
42450CB00005B/447